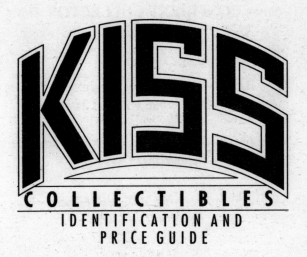

KISS

COLLECTIBLES

IDENTIFICATION AND
PRICE GUIDE

Other **CONFIDENT COLLECTOR** *Titles*
of Interest
from Avon Books

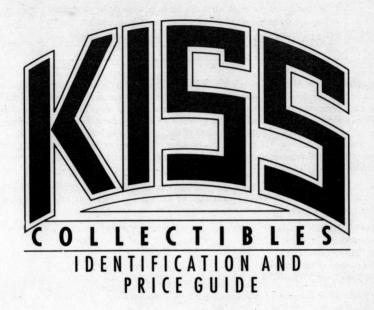

KISS

COLLECTIBLES
IDENTIFICATION AND
PRICE GUIDE

FIRST EDITION

KAREN AND JOHN LESNIEWSKI

The CONFIDENT COLLECTOR™

AVON BOOKS ◆ NEW YORK

THE CONFIDENT COLLECTOR: KISS COLLECTIBLES IDENTIFICATION AND PRICE GUIDE (1st Edition) is an original publication of Avon Books. This work has never before appeared in book form.

AVON BOOKS
A division of
The Hearst Corporation
1350 Avenue of the Americas
New York, New York 10019

Copyright © 1993 by John Lesniewski and Karen Lesniewski
Cover art by John and Karen Lesniewski
The Confident Collector and its logo are trademarked properties of Avon Books.
Interior design by Robin Arzt
Black-and-white photos courtesy of Heliochrome Productions
Published by arrangement with the authors
Library of Congress Catalog Card Number: 92-43828
ISBN: 0-380-77166-7

Library of Congress Cataloging in Publication Data:
Lesniewski, Karen.
   Kiss collectibles identification and price guide / Karen and John
Lesniewski.—1st ed.
      p.   cm.
   ''The Confident collector.''
   1. Kiss (Musical group)—Discography.   2. Kiss (Musical group)—
Collectibles—Catalogs.   I. Lesniewski, John.   II. Title.
ML156.7.K54L5   1993   92-43828
782.42166'092'2—dc20   CIP   MN

First Avon Books Trade Printing: June 1993

AVON TRADEMARK REG. U.S. PAT. OFF. AND IN OTHER COUNTRIES, MARCA REGISTRADA, HECHO EN U.S.A.

Printed in the U.S.A.

OPM   10   9   8   7   6   5   4   3   2

This book is dedicated to the memory of our beloved friend, Eric Carr, whose amazing drumming and wonderful personality will never be forgotten by anyone who knew him; and to the memory of Henry Wennmaker IV, who exemplified the term "die-hard KISS fan." We miss you both.

ACKNOWLEDGMENTS

Karen and John Lesniewski/The New England KISS Collectors' Network would like to thank the following people:

- Paul Stanley, Gene Simmons, Bruce Kulick, and Eric Singer for their music, their inspiration, and their constant support.

- Gilda Caserta for going above and beyond the call of duty, both as a professional and as a friend.

- Marcello Baca and all of the members of The New England KISS Collectors' Network all over the world, for their dedication.

- Lou Brutus, for being not only our favorite DJ, but a good friend and a true KISS fan.

- Our beautiful daughter, Angelina, and our parents, for everything.

- KISS fans everywhere, for keeping the faith.

The following people contributed to the research and production of this book: Marcello Baca, Gilda Caserta, Paul Scarborough, Mike Rutherford and Gina Parenti, Dave Thomas and Anders Holm (authors of *KISS Still On Fire*), *Goldmine* magazine and Neil Umphred, Dan Sherman, and the authors of *Hot Wacks*. Our special thanks and hellos also go out to: Ed VanDeWalle Jr.; Frank Hagan; Andy "But I got it from a reliable source!" Stern; Tom Valentino; Heath Kelley; Kevin "Aaaay" Talley; Kerry and Lisa DiGiandomenico; Kyle Joyce; Falk and Micki Friedrich; Russ at Quincy Records and Tapes in Quincy, Massachusetts; Holly and Tasos; John Langlois, Esquire, of Rhode Island, who provided our superb legal representation; Karen Shapiro at Avon Books; and Lasima, for all the times he faxed Gene for us! Thanks also to all the legitimate KISS fan clubs out there, the dedicated people who run them, and the die-hard fans who subscribe to KISS fanzines. . . . You keep the dream alive! Also thanks to Morrie and everyone at Rhymes Records at 59 Broadway in New Haven, CT, 06511 (203) 562-2508, for being a reliable supplier to KISS fans. Also Dave Henkel of Henkel Collectibles, 24 Orchard St., Ridgefield Park, NJ 07660, (201) 641-7212, who got us together with Avon Books. For more information on KISS magazines, see Dave Henkel's book, *The Confident Collector: Magazines, Identification and Price Guide*.

Special thanks to Play It Again Records, P.O. Box 418, Dewitt, NY 13214 . . . specializing in quality KISS collectibles.

And special thanks to Roni Feldman.

CONTENTS

KISS collecting is an exciting and virtually endless hobby, one that is growing in popularity all over the world. The only bands or artists who come close to KISS in merchandising are Elvis and the Beatles (although the New Kids on the Block are currently taking a shot at it). There is no need to make musical comparisons; Elvis is the King, the Beatles are the Fab Four, and KISS is the Hottest Band in the World.

As with any type of collecting, with more information, the hobby becomes easier and more fun. A price guide such as this one can help you identify the items that you find, list the items you still need to get, and help you determine how much you should pay for a particular item, depending on its condition. It's also an invaluable reference guide for anyone who sells KISS merchandise.

My husband, John, and I have been KISS fans since 1975 and 1978, respectively. In 1987 we held the first ever U.S. KISS convention in Boston, Massachusetts, and shortly thereafter started our fan club/newsletter, The New England KISS Collectors' Network. We began these projects in the hope of helping KISS fans and collectors like ourselves get together with fellow fans, keep up on the latest news about the band, and find merchandise to increase their collections. We now have hundreds of subscribers to the newsletter, and hundreds more KISS fans attend our conventions. Through the nine very successful KISS conventions we have held to date, we have learned a lot about KISS merchandise, and increased our personal KISS collection tremendously.

We have been collecting KISS memorabilia for many years, and we are considered by many fans and record dealers to be the experts on the value of KISS merchandise. Therefore, we felt it was our responsibility to put the information into a guide that would be useful to everyone, from brand-new fans to veteran collectors and record store owners.

One problem that we have noticed in the past is that there seemed to be regional fluctuations in the prices for KISS memorabilia. This was probably caused by the fact that the main concentration of KISS fans and collectors has always been in the northeastern United States, with large pockets in some areas (like Detroit) and a smaller percentage of KISS fans in the South and West. The numbers there are growing, but it still tends to be more difficult for people in those areas to find KISS merchandise. However, since collectors anywhere can easily buy KISS items through the mail from all parts of the country, these regional differences in price are unnecessary and can perhaps be eliminated by the publishing of this book. The values listed reflect the value of an item in stores in the Northeast and in mail-order ads from all parts of the country. However, the values are for buyers in the United States and Canada. Foreign collectors would pay more than these prices for American items, and they would pay less for items from their country than an American would. Foreign fans will have to use their judgment in deciding whether they are paying the right price for an item, but I hope that this guide will be helpful to them in learning what items are available.

Lastly, no list of KISS collectibles could ever truly be complete . . . at least, not a list that includes foreign items, promotional items, and even some bootleg items, as we have done here. So there will be items missing, but if you have any KISS items that are not listed in this book, we would appreciate it if you would contact us. If we need a photograph of the item, we will ask you to provide one for future editions of this book. Also, anyone interested in subscribing to our KISS newsletter should send us a stamped, self-addressed, business-size envelope. All correspondence and subscription inquiries should be sent to:

The New England KISS Collectors' Network
168 Oakland Avenue, Providence, RI 02908 U.S.A.

We can also be reached *between 10:00 A.M. and 8:00 P.M. Eastern Time* at the following number: (401) 273-4246. Please bear in mind that we cannot return long-distance calls.

Thank you for purchasing this book, and we hope you enjoy it!

Karen Lesniewski
The New England KISS Collectors' Network

THE
MUSIC

RATINGS FOR VINYL ALBUMS: *(For ratings in between these, use + or —)*

Mint: Untouched, pristine. Refers to an album that is completely free of scratches, ringwear, or any other flaw. A "mint" record should look as if it just came from the pressing plant.

Excellent (EX): Very close to mint, but not absolutely perfect. Slight surface scratches on the record that don't affect play, or slight scuffs on the cover, are acceptable in this rating, but skips or major scratches, or creases in the cover, are not.

Very Good (VG): In general, records in this rating may have some small scratches, but should still play well. Covers may have some minor damage (small scuffs or slight ringwear, corners slightly bent, or small rips in the inner sleeve), but should not be in "beat-up" shape.

Good: Slight scratches on the record, surface noise, but playable. Bent corners or large scratches or tears on the cover. Major damage to the inner sleeve.

Fair: Definitely damaged in some way: skips or big scratches in the record, major cover damage and/or ringwear, inner sleeve badly ripped or missing.

Poor: Terrible shape; record unplayable, and cover very damaged.

Cover: The cardboard outer sleeve of a vinyl album; also, the artwork on the cover.

Cut Corner: A record with one corner cut off of the cover. This is often done to records when they are put into bargain-price bins, are sold at a discount as overstock, or are given away as promos. The practice is intended to keep people from returning a record for a full-price refund when they didn't pay full price for it.

45 Sleeve: The paper sleeve that 7-inch records come in. See also *picture sleeve.*

Gatefold: An album cover that opens up, such as *Alive II.*

Inner Sleeve: The paper sleeve between a record album and the cover.

Insert: Any item that was put into a record jacket as a gift to the purchaser, such as a photo booklet. Inner sleeves do not count as inserts.

Label: The paper sticker on the center of a vinyl record, which contains the pertinent information about the record.

Label Hole: A hole in a record sleeve or cover that allows only the label to be seen.

Misprint: Any record cover, sleeve, or label that was printed incorrectly and/or is different from the majority of copies of that record. For example, if most copies of an album list a song as "I Still Love You," but you find a copy that lists it as "I Still Leave You," that is a misprint.

Picture Sleeve: A paper sleeve for a 7-inch record that is printed with a picture or information about the song/artist, as opposed to a basic record-company sleeve. Picture sleeves generally do not have label holes.

Promo or **Promotional Item:** An item originally given to a radio station or record store to promote the band. Although not intended for sale, they are common collector's items.

Ringwear: The white scuffs on a record cover where the edges of the record press against the cover. Ringwear dramatically reduces the value of the record.

7-Inch Hole/12-Inch Hole: A hole in a record cover or sleeve that allows you to see the whole record. Usually only used for picture discs.

White Label: A special promotional label that is white and differs from the label on regular copies of the record. Also used to denote the blank white label sometimes used on test pressings. Many promotional albums do not have white labels.

HISTORY OF THE RECORD LABELS

In order to collect KISS records, a fan must be able to distinguish between 1st and later pressings. This requires a working knowledge of the different Casablanca and Mercury/Polygram labels. Descriptions and examples of the labels used on KISS records follow.

CASABLANCA LABELS

Casablanca Label #1
Description: Blue/gray label with red Casablanca logo, and with "mfd. and dist. by Warner" at bottom.
Note: Used in 1974 on #9000 series. (The first KISS album, without "Kissing Time," is Serial #9001.)
Used for: *KISS*, very first pressing, *without* "Kissing Time."

Casablanca label #1

Casablanca label #1a

Casablanca Label #1a
Description: Blue/gray label, red Casablanca logo, with "mfd. and dist. by Casablanca" printed at bottom without street address.
Note: Used in 1974, 1975, and the first part of 1976.
Used for: *KISS* (with "Kissing Time") through *Alive!*

Casablanca Label #1b
Description: Same as Casablanca Label #1a, except with "8255 Sunset Blvd." added at bottom.
Note: Brief transitional label used in mid-1976.
Used for: *Destroyer.*

Casablanca Label #2
Description: Color picture label, beige, with 3 camels in view.
Note: Used from mid-1976 (approximately from Serial #7026) to mid-1977 (approximately to Serial #7050).
Used for: *The Originals* and *Rock and Roll Over.*

Casablanca Label #3
Description: Color picture label, beige; same scene as Label #2, except with "film crew" added; "Casablanca Records" is printed at bottom. "Casablanca Records" logo at top has been changed to "Casablanca Records and Film-works."
Note: Used from mid-1977 (approximately from Serial #7054) to early 1981 (approximately to Serial #7255).
Used for: *Love Gun* (also had *Love Gun* cover picture on label), *Alive II*, *Double Platinum* (with silver bottom half of label), and the solo albums (with each member's face on his label).

Casablanca Label #3a
Description: Same as Label #3, except with "Polygram Records" at bottom.
Note: Used from 1981 until Casablanca labels were phased out.
Used for: *Creatures of the Night* 2nd pressing (1st pressing used special black label with silver KISS logo), and later Polygram pressings of the early albums.

Casablanca label #1b

Casablanca label #2

Casablanca label #3

Casablanca label #3a

MERCURY/POLYGRAM LABELS

Mercury Label #1
Description: Black label with large red Mercury logo. Fine print reads, "Manufactured and Marketed by Polygram Records, Inc."
Note: Used from 1983 to 1989.
Used for: *Lick It Up, Animalize, Asylum, Crazy Nights*, and *Smashes, Thrashes, and Hits*. Also used for 3rd pressing of *Creatures of the Night* (with non-makeup cover).

Mercury Label #1a
Description: Black label with large red Mercury logo. Fine print reads, "Manufactured and Marketed by Polygram Records, Inc., New York, New York. All rights reserved. Unauthorized copying, reproduction, hiring, lending, public performance and broadcasting prohibited. Printed in USA."
Note: Used in 1989.
Used for: *Hot in the Shade.* (*Hot in the Shade* was the last KISS album released on vinyl in the United States.)

SPECIAL KISS LABELS

Love Gun: Same as Casablanca Label #3, except with picture of band (from cover) printed over camel picture.
Double Platinum: Casablanca Label #3 with silver bottom half. Top reads, "Casablanca Records and Filmworks [logo] Honors KISS [silver KISS logo]."
Solo LPs: Same as Casablanca Label #3, except with picture of each KISS member (from cover) printed on his label.
Dynasty: Bottom half of label is white, and the top half is the photograph from the poster that originally came with the album. Small red "Casablanca Records and Filmworks" logo is under song credits.
Unmasked: Bottom half of label is white, and the top half is the illustration from the cover showing KISS removing their masks.
The Elder: Picture label (from front cover of LP, photo of Paul's hand reaching for door knocker). Fine print reads, "Manufactured and Marketed by Polygram Records, Inc."
Creatures: (1st pressing only) Plain black label with large silver KISS logo.

PROMOTIONAL LABELS

During the age of vinyl albums, free copies to be sent to radio stations (promotional albums) generally had a different label than the albums released to the general public. Often the only difference was the phrase "Promotional Copy—Not For

Mercury label #1

Mercury label #1a

Love Gun label

Double Platinum label

Sale" on the label. Other promotional albums had special white labels to denote their status as promotional items. Sometimes the LP cover would have a gold stamp on it that said "Promotional Copy—Not For Sale." (Occasionally "promo" albums also had a white sticker on the front of the album cover listing all the songs, their length, and how much time the disc jockey had to talk before the singing started. These stickers were never used on KISS albums, however.) Some promotional albums also had a notch cut into the album cover, or had one corner cut off, to denote that they were promotional, but not all so-called cut-corner albums are promotional. Corner cutting was also used by stores when albums were sold in bargain bins, the idea being that it would keep people from buying an album at a reduced price, then returning it for full price.

Dynasty label

Unmasked label

Mercury label #1

Mercury label #1a

Love Gun label

The solo-LP labels are Casablanca Label #3 with the individual member's photo on the label.

Double Platinum label

(Music from) The Elder label

Creatures of the Night label

"THE ORIGINALS"

KISS

NBLP 7032 A
(7032-3-998-1A)

SIDE 1
STEREO
Promotion Copy
Not For Sale

*1. STRUTTER (Stanley/Simmons)   3:10
2. NOTHIN' TO LOSE (Simmons)   3:26
3. FIREHOUSE (Stanley)   3:18
*4. COLD GIN (Frehley)   4:21
5. LET ME KNOW (Stanley)   2:58

Prod. by Kenny Kerner and Richie Wise
All selections published by Cafe Americana Inc./
Rock Steady Music, ASCAP, except
*as indicated, also Co-published by
Gladwyne Music Publishing Corp.
©1974, 1976 Casablanca
Records, Inc.

An example of a "white label." This term is
used for special white promotional labels.
KISS used white labels only on promotional
copies of *KISS* and *The Originals.*

45 label for "Flaming Youth"

Promotional 45 label for "Flaming Youth"
(note the words "Promotion/Not for Sale")

Promotional "gold stamp." These are
hot-stamped onto some promotional
album covers.

U.S. LPs

(Prices for U.S. LPs can be found beginning on page 39)

Album: *KISS*
Released: 2/74
Serial #: NB9001; NBLP7001
Labels:
    1st Pressing (without "Kissing Time"): Casablanca Label #1
    2nd Pressing (with "Kissing Time"): Casablanca Label #1a
    3rd Pressing: Casablanca Label #2
    4th Pressing: Casablanca Label #3
    5th Pressing: Casablanca Label #3a
Inserts: No inserts.
Special Notations: Very 1st pressing of the LP did not include the song "Kissing
    Time" and had Serial #NB9001. All pressings with "Kissing Time" are Serial
    #NBLP7001. The 5th pressing, a Mercury/Polygram re-release, has a UPC
    symbol on the cover and has a live version of "Nothin' to Lose" instead of the
    original version.

KISS (1st album), front and back covers

Album: *Hotter Than Hell*
Released: 10/74
Serial #: NBLP7006
Labels:
   1st Pressing: Casablanca Label #1a
   2nd Pressing: Casablanca Label #2
   3rd Pressing: Casablanca Label #3
   4th Pressing: Casablanca Label #3a
Inserts: No inserts.
Special Notations: Very slight variations of color exist between the 1st and 2nd pressing covers. (Check red/silver border.) The 4th pressing is a Mercury re-release with a UPC symbol.

Album: *Dressed to Kill*
Released: 3/75
Serial #: NBLP7016
Labels:
   1st Pressing: Casablanca Label #1a
   2nd Pressing: Casablanca Label #2
   3rd Pressing: Casablanca Label #3
   4th Pressing: Casablanca Label #3a
Inserts: No inserts.
Special Notations: The first 3 pressings (the Casablanca pressings) had raised letters on the cover (the black KISS logos). The 4th pressing (a Mercury/Polygram re-release) does not, and it has a UPC symbol on the back of the cover.

Hotter Than Hell, front and back covers

Dressed to Kill, front and back covers

Album: *Alive!*
Released: 9/75
Serial #: NBLP7020
Labels:
    1st Pressing: Casablanca Label #1a
    2nd Pressing: Casablanca Label #2
    3rd Pressing: Casablanca Label #3
    4th Pressing: Casablanca Label #3a
Inserts: 8-page color booklet (12 by 12 inches) with pictures of KISS from 1974 and 1975.
Special Notations: Gatefold cover. The 2nd, 3rd, and 4th pressings say "A 2-Record Set" on the front cover. The 4th pressing cover is not gatefold.

Alive!, front, back, and inside covers

Alive!, front and inside of booklet

Album: *Destroyer*
Released: 3/76
Serial #: NBLP7025
Labels:
  1st Pressing: Casablanca Label #1a
  2nd Pressing: Casablanca Label #2
  3rd Pressing: Casablanca Label #3
  4th Pressing: Casablanca Label #3a
Inserts: No inserts.
Special Notations: In first 3 pressings, inner sleeve is thin cardboard, black, with the KISS Army logo on one side and the words "Detroit Rock City" on the other. The 1st-pressing inner sleeve opens at the side, and later-pressing inner sleeves open at the top. The 4th pressing had a plain white sleeve. Also, the printing on the promotional label is different from the printing on the regular (non-promo) 1st-pressing label.

Destroyer, front and back covers, and front and back inner sleeves

Also, on the first 2 pressings of the LP, after "Do You Love Me," there is a short, distorted recording of Paul (from *Alive!*) saying, "We're gonna have ourselves . . . a rock and roll party!" It repeats several times, echoing and fading. (Interestingly enough, although Polygram did not put this on their later pressings of the LP, they did put it on the CD version of *Destroyer.*)

Album: *The Originals*
Released: 7/76
Serial #: NBLP7032; NBLP7032-2
Labels:
　　1st Pressing (Serial #NBLP7032): Casablanca Label #2
　　2nd Pressing (Serial #NBLP7032–2): Casablanca Label #3
Inserts: A sheet of 6 perforated KISS trading cards (different from the Donruss series of KISS cards), a KISS Army sticker, and an 11-by-11-inch 16-page booklet. The booklet has a sepia-toned (brownish) cover showing an early KISS concert poster which says, "Rock and Roll Ball With KISS."

The Originals, front and back covers

The Originals, inside cover and inner sleeves. The inner sleeves are printed to look like the covers of the first three KISS albums.

Inserts from _The Originals_: booklet, KISS Army sticker, and set of perforated KISS cards

Special Notations: "Bookfold" cover (similar to a gatefold, but albums can be lifted out from center). _The Originals_ was a special repackaging of the first 3 albums. The inner sleeves look like the covers of _KISS, Hotter Than Hell,_ and _Dressed to Kill_. In the 1st pressing, the inner sleeves have a dull finish; in the 2nd pressing, they're glossy. There were only 2 pressings ever made, and the 2nd has "Second Pressing" printed right on the front cover.

Album: _Rock and Roll Over_
Released: 11/76
Serial #: NBLP7037
Labels:
    1st Pressing: Casablanca Label #2
    2nd Pressing: Casablanca Label #3
    3rd Pressing: Casablanca Label #3a
Inserts: Square 13-piece sticker of _Rock and Roll Over_ cover, and merchandise order form.
Special Notations: In first 2 (Casablanca) pressings, inner sleeve is black with orange KISS logos and lightning bolts on it.

Rock and Roll Over, front and back covers

Inserts from *Rock and Roll Over*: inner sleeve, merchandise order form, and sticker

Love Gun, front and back covers

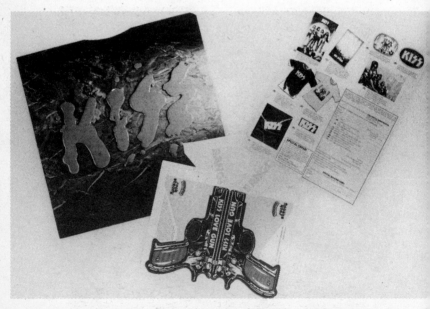

Inserts from *Love Gun:* inner sleeve, merchandise order form, and "Love Gun" (bottom)

Album: *Love Gun*
Released: 6/77
Serial #: NBLP7057
Labels:
 1st Pressing: Love Gun Label
 2nd Pressing: Casablanca Label #3a
Inserts: (1st pressing only) The infamous "Love Gun." It was a cardboard gun that would make a popping noise when opened. It came on a single thin cardboard sheet, perforated for removal. The "gun" is worth more if it is unassembled. There was also a merchandise order form in *Love Gun.*
Special Notations: The 1st pressing has a green inner sleeve with "KISS" written on it in "blood."

Album: *Alive II*
Released: 10/77
Serial #: NBLP7076–2
Labels:
 1st Pressing: Casablanca Label #3
 2nd Pressing: Casablanca Label #3a

Alive II, front, back, and inside covers

Inserts from *Alive II*: booklet, inner sleeve, "tattoos," and merchandise order form

Inserts: Full-color 8-page booklet (11 by 11 inches) with pictures of KISS from 1973 to 1978, a set of KISS rub-on "tattoos," and a merchandise order form.

Special Notations: Gatefold. Inner sleeves show a crowd of fans at a KISS concert on one side, and all the KISS albums up to that point on the other side.

Album: *Double Platinum*
Released: 4/78
Serial #: NBLP7100–2
Labels:
  1st Pressing: Double Platinum Label
  2nd Pressing: Casablanca Label #3a
  3rd Pressing: Casablanca Label #3a
Inserts: (1st pressing only) "Platinum Plaque." This was a thin cardboard replica of a platinum album award with a space for the fan's name. There was also a merchandise order form in *Double Platinum*.
Special Notations: The 1st and 2nd pressings have a gatefold cover with raised silver KISS logos. The 3rd pressing is not gatefold and has a flat grayish cover with a UPC symbol on the back. Although the 1st pressing always had the Double Platinum Label, we have seen it with the words typeset three different ways; these are probably all 1st pressings, but were manufactured in different places.

Double Platinum cover, "plaque," and merchandise order form

Double Platinum inside covers

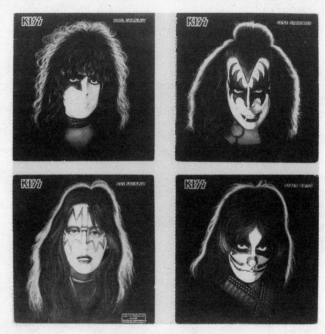

The KISS solo albums, front covers

Album: *Paul Stanley*
Released: 9/78
Serial #: NBLP7123

Album: *Gene Simmons*
Released: 9/78
Serial #: NBLP7120

Album: *Ace Frehley*
Released: 9/78
Serial #: NBLP7121

Album: *Peter Criss*
Released: 9/78
Serial #: NBLP7122
Labels:
    1st Pressing: Solo Album Labels
    2nd Pressing: Casablanca Label #3a

The KISS solo albums, back covers

Inserts: (1st pressing only) Each solo LP contained an illustrated poster of the KISS member whose album it was, and the 4 posters fit together to form one giant poster. Also, each solo LP has a different merchandise order form (Paul Stanley's having Paul merchandise, etc.), and Peter Criss's album also contained a paper sheet with information about his album.

Special Notation: Inner sleeves for all solo LPs show the covers of all 4 solo LPs. Also, there are solo LPs with different printing on the labels, so there may have been several Casablanca pressings. The Mercury/Polygram pressing is easy to spot, as it has the UPC symbol on the back of the album.

Album: *Dynasty*
Released: 5/79
Serial #: NBLP7152
Labels:
    1st Pressing: Dynasty Label
    2nd Pressing: Casablanca Label #3a

The posters from Paul's and Gene's solo albums

The posters from Peter's and Ace's solo albums

Inserts from the solo albums: inner sleeve and the four different merchandise order forms (one from each album)

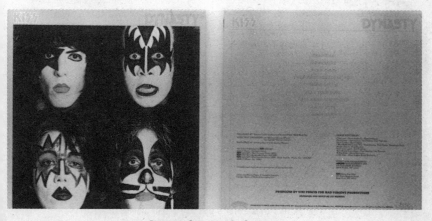

Dynasty, front and back covers

Inserts from *Dynasty*: poster, inner sleeve, and merchandise order form

Inserts: Poster of KISS with gray background. Also, merchandise order form.
Special Notations: (1st pressing only) Inner sleeve has multicolored logos over-lapping each other. The Mercury/Polygram pressing (2nd pressing) has a UPC symbol on the back of the cover.

Album: *Unmasked*
Released: 5/80
Serial #: NBLP7225
Labels:
    1st Pressing: Unmasked Label
    2nd Pressing: Casablanca Label #3a
Inserts: (1st pressing only) Poster of the illustrated panel of KISS taking off masks, from the front cover of the LP. Also, a merchandise order form.
Special Notations: Inner sleeve was a plain black glossy sleeve with a label hole in the middle. The Mercury/Polygram pressing (2nd pressing) has a UPC symbol on the back of the cover.

Unmasked, front and back covers

Inserts from *Unmasked*: poster and merchandise order form

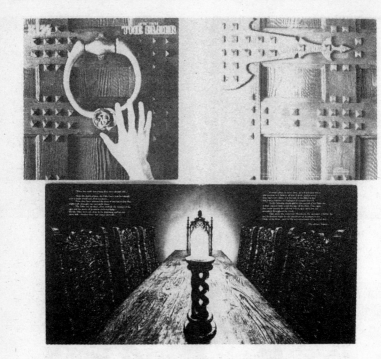

(Music from) **The Elder, front, back, and inside covers**

Album: *(Music from) The Elder*
Released: 11/81
Serial #: NBLP7261
Labels:
    All pressings: The Elder Label
Inserts: Some pressings contained a separate lyric sheet (glossy white paper with black ink).
Special Notations: There are at least 2 different covers and 2 inner sleeves for *The Elder*, and only some copies have the insert, which leads us to believe that this album was pressed in several places at once. Some covers have the songs in the correct order on the back cover, but most have the songs listed in a different order. Most copies had an inner sleeve that was clear plastic with credits on it, but there were some copies that had a paper inner sleeve with the lyrics on it. Copies with the lyrics on the inner sleeve or on the separate piece of paper are somewhat rarer than the copies with no lyrics. All *Elder* covers are gatefold.

(Music from) The Elder **alternate back cover, lyric sheet, paper inner sleeve with lyrics, and clear plastic inner sleeve**

Album: *Creatures of the Night*
Released: 10/82
Serial #: NBLP7270
Labels:
    1st Pressing: Creatures Label
    2nd Pressing: Casablanca Label #3 (Fine print: "53Manufactured and Marketed by Polygram Records, Inc.")
    3rd Pressing (1985 reprinting with non-makeup cover): Mercury Label #2
Inserts: None
Special Notations: *Creatures of the Night* had 2 very different covers. The 1st was a shot of Paul's, Gene's, Ace's, and Eric Carr's faces in makeup, with a blue background. This cover was used for the first 2 pressings, and you can tell the difference between the 2 covers, because the 1st pressing has the number 501 printed on the upper right corner of the back cover, and the 2nd pressing has a UPC *sticker* on the cover.

    The 2nd cover, used for the 3rd pressing in 1985, was a non-makeup

Creatures of the Night **front and back covers, inner sleeve, and second cover (reissue cover, without makeup)**

photo of Gene, Paul, Eric Carr, and Bruce Kulick, with an orange background. The 3rd pressing (2nd cover) has the UPC symbol printed right on the cover.

The inner sleeves of the 1st and 2nd pressings were a black paper sleeve with the lyrics printed in white. Inner sleeves used for the 3rd pressing were either a clear plastic sleeve or a paper sleeve similar to the one in the original pressing.

Album: *Lick It Up*
Released: 9/83
Serial #: 422–814 297–1 M–1
Labels:
    1st Pressing: Mercury Label #1
Inserts: None
Special Notations: Inner sleeve is white with lyrics in black. In some pressings, sleeve is glossy; in others, it's a dull (matte) finish. UPC symbol on the back of the cover.

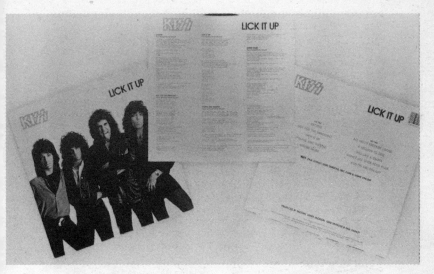

Lick It Up front cover, inner sleeve, and back cover

Album: *Animalize*
Released: 9/84
Serial #: 422–822 495–1 M–1
Labels:
 1st Pressing: Mercury Label #2
Inserts: None
Special Notations: Inner sleeve is white with lyrics on one side, and photo of the band (Gene, Paul, Eric Carr, Mark St. John) on the other side. In some pressings, sleeve is glossy; in others, it has a dull (matte) finish. UPC symbol on the back of the cover.

Album: *Asylum*
Released: 9/85
Serial #: 422–826 099–1 M–1
Labels:
 1st Pressing: Mercury Label #2
Inserts: None
Special Notations: Inner sleeve is white with lyrics. Down the sides of the inner sleeves are photo strips of each member of the band (Paul, Gene, Eric Carr, Bruce). UPC symbol on the back of the cover.

Animalize front cover, inner sleeve, and back cover

Asylum front cover, inner sleeve, and back cover

Crazy Nights **front cover, inner sleeve, and back cover**

Album: *Crazy Nights*
Released: 9/87
Serial #: 422 832 626–1 Q–1
Labels:
>   1st Pressing: Mercury Label #2

Inserts: None
Special Notations: Inner sleeve is white with lyrics on one side, and photo of
the band (Gene, Paul, Eric Carr, Bruce) on the other side. UPC symbol on the
back of the cover.

Album: *Smashes, Thrashes, and Hits*
Released: 11/88
Serial #: 422 836 427–1
Labels:
>   1st Pressing: Mercury Label #2

Inserts: None
Special Notations: Inner sleeve is white with lyrics. UPC symbol on the back of
the cover. Also, the song "Rock and Roll All Nite" is changed to "Rock and
Roll All *Night*" on this album. (Perhaps KISS decided that spelling counts after
all!)

Smashes, Thrashes, and Hits front cover, inner sleeve, and back cover

Hot in the Shade front cover, inner sleeve, and back cover

Album: *Hot in the Shade*
Released: 10/89
Serial #: 422 838 913-1 Q-1
Labels:
　　1st Pressing: Mercury Label #2
Inserts: None
Special Notations: Inner sleeve is white with lyrics. UPC symbol on the back of
　　the cover.

Album: *Revenge*
Released: 5/92
Serial #: 848 037-2
Revenge was never released on vinyl in the United States. (See "Foreign LPs" or
"CDs and Laserdiscs")

U.S. LP VALUES

　　This section lists approximate values for U.S. vinyl LPs,
depending on condition and other factors. The values listed are
for mint (that is, perfect) copies, so you should pay less than the
following amounts listed for a copy that is not mint. In some
cases, a mint 1st pressing is worth the same or more than a sealed
copy because those albums' covers are identical in the 1st and
2nd pressing; thus, in those cases, there is no way to prove that
a sealed copy is a 1st pressing. Such albums are marked with an
asterisk next to the value of a sealed copy.

Album	Original Label, Sealed	Original with Inserts	Original without Inserts	Promo Copy	2nd Pressing with Inserts	Additional Pressing without Inserts
KISS	without "Kissing Time" $65	No inserts	without "Kissing Time" $55	White Label $75	No inserts	2nd-$15 3rd-$10 4th-$8

cont.

Album	Original Label, Sealed	Original with Inserts	Original without Inserts	Promo Copy	2nd Pressing with Inserts	Additional Pressing without Inserts
Hotter Than Hell	$12*	No inserts	$15	$20	No inserts	2nd–$8 3rd–$5
Dressed to Kill	$12*	No inserts	$15	$20	No inserts	2nd–$8 3rd–$5
Alive!	$25	$20	$12	$35	$12	$8
Destroyer	$12*	No inserts	$15	$20	No inserts	$7
The Originals	$100	with all $90	$60	White Label $125	with all $85	$55
Rock and Roll Over	$10*	$12	$9	$20	$9	$6
Love Gun	$10*	$25; if gun is made, $18	$8	$20	No inserts/ 2nd press.	$5
Alive II	$15*	$18	$10	$35	$15	$7
Double Platinum	$12*	$15	$8	$25	No inserts/ 2nd press.	$6
Solo LPs	$12	$10	$6	$18	No inserts/ 2nd press.	$4

Album	Original Label, Sealed	Original with Inserts	Original without Inserts	Promo Copy	2nd Pressing with Inserts	Additional Pressing without Inserts
Dynasty	$12	$10	$6	$20	No inserts/ 2nd press.	$4
Unmasked	$12	$10	$6	$20	No inserts/ 2nd press.	$4
(Music from) The Elder	$35	$30 (with lyrics)	$25	$50	No 2nd press.	No 2nd press.
Creatures of the Night	$30	No inserts	$25	$35	No inserts	2nd–$20 3rd–$6
Lick It Up	$10	No inserts	$7	$15	No 2nd press.	No 2nd press.
Animalize	$10	No inserts	$7	$15	No 2nd press.	No 2nd press.
Asylum	$10	No inserts	$6	$15	No 2nd press.	No 2nd press.
Crazy Nights	$10	No inserts	$6	$15	No 2nd press.	No 2nd press.
Smashes, Thrashes, and Hits	$10	No inserts	$6	$15	No 2nd press.	No 2nd press.
Hot in the Shade	$10	No inserts	$6	$15	No 2nd press.	No 2nd press.

FOREIGN PRESSINGS OF U.S. RELEASES

Use these groupings with the following chart to determine the approximate value of an original pressing of a particular LP from a particular country. The value would be slightly higher if the album was gatefold from that country, but was not a gatefold in the U.S., or if it had interesting inserts, or if the cover art is different from that of U.S. copies. For promotional pressings, add $5 per disc. NR means Not Released.

Group A: KISS, Hotter Than Hell, Dressed to Kill, Alive!, Destroyer, Rock and Roll Over, Love Gun, Alive II, Double Platinum
Group B: The Originals
Group C: Four Solo LPs (Paul Stanley, Gene Simmons, Ace Frehley, Peter Criss), Dynasty, Unmasked
Group D: The Elder, Creatures of the Night (1st cover)
Group E: Creatures of the Night (2nd cover), Lick It Up, Animalize, Asylum, Crazy Nights, Smashes, Thrashes and Hits, Hot in the Shade, Revenge

Country	A	B	C	D	E
Australia	$25	N/R	$25	$30	$20
Brazil, Portugal, Mexico, Argentina	$30	N/R	$25	$40	$25
Canada	$20	$115	$15	$20	$12
England, France, Spain, Greece, Italy, The Netherlands	$25	N/R	$25	$30	$15
Germany (assuming German logo)	$20	N/R	$20	$30	$15
Israel, Saudi Arabia	$30	N/R	$25	$30	$25
Taiwan	$30	N/R	$30	$35	$30
Japan	$35	$160	$35	$40	$30

Hotter Than Hell from three different countries: (l. to r.) Germany, Argentina, and Japan

These albums were released only outside the U.S. Top left, *The Originals II,* from Japan. Top right, *Killers,* from Germany (*Killers* was also released in some other European countries, Argentina, and in Australia). Bottom left, *Superstar,* from Italy. Bottom right, *Hotter Than Metal,* from England.

FOREIGN RELEASES

Originals II: A special repackaging of *Destroyer*, *Rock and Roll Over*, and *Love Gun*, similar in style to *The Originals*. Comes with 4 cardboard cartoon "masks" of the original members, a black-and-white lyric booklet, and a color photo booklet. Only released in Japan.

> With all inserts: $275–300
> Without inserts: $175–200

Killers: Greatest-hits compilation with 4 new songs. It was released in Europe, Argentina, Australia, and Japan, but the Japanese pressing includes "Shandi" and "Escape from the Island," and the Australian pressing includes "Shandi" and "Talk to Me," which are not on the European pressings. No inserts. Of the European pressings, the German ones were released with the German logo, and the other European pressings have the regular logo. Because it wasn't released in the United States, many European copies were imported to the U.S. and are fairly easy to find. *Killers* is also available on CD from Japan.

> European LP: $5–10
> Argentinian LP: $25–30
> Australian LP: $25–30
> Japanese LP: $25–30
> Japanese CD: $35–40

Hotter Than Metal: Not an official release but licensed by Polygram, this album contains Sides One and Two of *Alive!* and has a color cover. It was released in Europe, but some copies have been imported to the United States. $15–18

Superstar: Also not official, but licensed. This is also Sides One and Two of *Alive!*, but the cover is gatefold with a full-color booklet. (The booklet is written in Italian, and refers to Eric Carr as "Edwin Carr".) This was only released in Italy, but some copies have been imported to the U.S. $18–22

Chikara: Greatest-hits compilation released only in Japan, and *only* on CD. Some came with a patch of the Chikara symbol.

> With patch: $40–45
> Without patch: $35–40

U.S. 45s

The following is the complete list of 7-inch vinyl 45s released by KISS in the United States, along with the serial number, year released, and the values for the regular 45 and the promotional copy. If the 45 came with a picture sleeve, the value listed is for the sleeve *and* record, not for the sleeve alone. In general, KISS collectors are not as apt to collect empty picture sleeves as other collectors are, but if you want to know the value of an empty KISS picture sleeve, subtract the regular 45 value from the picture-sleeve-with-record value. Values here assume mint/EX condition.

A-side/B-side

"Nothin' to Lose"/
"Love Theme from KISS"
   Serial #: NEB0004
   Released: 1974
   7-inch vinyl 45: $7
   No picture sleeve
   Promotional copy: $10
"Kissin' Time"/"Nothin' to Lose"
   Serial #: NEB0011
   Released: 1974
   7-inch vinyl 45: $7
   No picture sleeve
   Promotional copy: $10
"Strutter"/"100,000 Years"
   Serial #: NEB0015
   Released: 1974
   7-inch vinyl 45: $7
   No picture sleeve
   Promotional copy: $10
"Let Me Go, Rock 'N' Roll"/
"Hotter Than Hell"
   Serial #: NB823
   Released: 1974
   7-inch vinyl 45: $7
   No picture sleeve
   Promotional copy: $10

A-side/B-side

"Rock and Roll All Nite"/"Getaway"
   Serial #: NB829
   Released: 1975
   7-inch vinyl 45: $7
   No picture sleeve
   Promotional copy: $10
"C'mon and Love Me"/"Getaway"
   Serial #: NB841
   Released: 1975
   7-inch vinyl 45: $7
   No picture sleeve
   Promotional copy: $10
"Rock and Roll All Nite"
(Live version)/(studio version)
   Serial #: NB850
   Released: 1975
   7-inch vinyl 45: $6
   No picture sleeve
   Promotional copy: $8
"Shout It Out Loud"/"Sweet Pain"
   Serial #: NB854
   Released: 1976
   7-inch vinyl 45: $7
   No picture sleeve
   Promotional copy: $10

"Flaming Youth"/"God of Thunder"
  Serial #: NB858
  Released: 1976
  7-inch vinyl 45: $8
  With picture sleeve: $15
  Promotional copy: $12

"Detroit Rock City"/"Beth"
  Serial #: NB863
  Released: 1976
  7-inch vinyl 45: $6
  No picture sleeve
  Promotional copy: $8

"Beth"/"Detroit Rock City"
  Serial #: NB863
  Released: 1976
  7-inch vinyl 45: $6
  No picture sleeve
  Promotional copy: $8

"Hard Luck Woman"/"Mr. Speed"
  Serial #: NB873
  Released: 1976
  7-inch vinyl 45: $5
  No picture sleeve
  Promotional copy: $7

"Calling Dr. Love"/"Take Me"
  Serial #: NB880
  Released: 1977
  7-inch vinyl 45: $5
  No picture sleeve
  Promotional copy: $7

"Christine Sixteen"/"Shock Me"
  Serial #: NB889
  Released: 1977
  7-inch vinyl 45: $5
  No picture sleeve
  Promotional copy: $7

"Love Gun"/"Hooligan"
  Serial #: NB895
  Released: 1977
  7-inch vinyl 45: $5
  No picture sleeve
  Promotional copy: $7

"Shout It Out Loud" (live)/
"Nothin' to Lose"
  Serial #: NB906
  Released: 1978
  7-inch vinyl 45: $5
  No picture sleeve
  Promotional copy: $7

"Rocket Ride"/
"Tomorrow and Tonight"
  Serial #: NB915
  Released: 1978
  7-inch vinyl 45: $5
  No picture sleeve
  Promotional copy: $7

"Strutter '78"/"Shock Me"
  Serial #: NB928
  Released: 1978
  7-inch vinyl 45: $6
  No picture sleeve
  Promotional copy: $8

"Hold Me, Touch Me"/"Goodbye"
  (P. Stanley)
  Serial #: NB940
  Released: 1978
  7-inch vinyl 45: $6
  No picture sleeve
  Promotional copy: $8

"New York Groove"/"Snow Blind"
  (A. Frehley)
  Serial #: NB941
  Released: 1978
  7-inch vinyl 45: $6
  No picture sleeve
  Promotional copy: $8

"Radioactive"/
"See You in Your Dreams"
  (G. Simmons)
  Serial #: NB951
  Released: 1978
  7-inch vinyl 45: $6
  No picture sleeve
  Promotional copy: $8

U.S. 45s: These are the seven picture-sleeve 45s
released in the U.S.

"Don't You Let Me Down"/
"Hooked On Rock and Roll"
    (P. Criss)
    Serial #: NB952
    Released: 1978
    7-inch vinyl 45: $6
    No picture sleeve
    Promotional copy: $8

"You Still Matter to Me"/
"Hooked on Rock and Roll"
    (P. Criss)
    Serial #: NB961
    Released: 1978
    7-inch vinyl 45: $7
    No picture sleeve
    Promotional copy: $8

"I Was Made for Lovin' You"/
"Hard Times"
    Serial #: NB983
    Released: 1979
    7-inch vinyl 45: $5
    No picture sleeve
    Promotional copy: $7

"Sure Know Something"/
"Dirty Livin'"
    Serial #: NB2205
    Released: 1979
    7-inch vinyl 45: $5
    No picture sleeve
    Promotional copy: $7

"Shandi"/"She's So European"
    Serial #: NB2282
    Released: 1980
    7-inch vinyl 45: $6
    No picture sleeve
    Promotional copy: $8

"Tomorrow"/"Naked City"
    Serial #: NB2299
    Released: 1980
    7-inch vinyl 45: $6
    No picture sleeve
    Promotional copy: $8

"A World Without Heroes"/
"Dark Light"
    Serial #: NB2343
    Released: 1981
    7-inch vinyl 45: $7
    No picture sleeve
    Promotional copy: $10

"I Love It Loud"/"Danger"
    Serial #: NB2365
    Released: 1982
    7-inch vinyl 45: $8
    With picture sleeve: $15
    Promotional copy: $10

"Lick It Up"/
"Dance All Over Your Face"
    Serial #: 814 671
    Released: 1983
    7-inch vinyl 45: $4
    No picture sleeve
    Promotional copy: $7

"All Hell's Breakin' Loose"/
"Young and Wasted"
    Serial #: 818 216
    Released: 1983
    7-inch vinyl 45: $4
    No picture sleeve
    Promotional copy: $7

"Heaven's on Fire"/
"Lonley Is the Hunter"
    Serial #: 880 205
    Released: 1984
    7-inch vinyl 45: $4
    No picture sleeve
    Promotional copy: $7

"Thrills in the Night"/
"Burn, Bitch, Burn"
    Serial #: 880 535
    Released: 1984
    7-inch vinyl 45: $4
    No picture sleeve
    Promotional copy: $7

"Tears Are Falling"/
"Any Way You Slice It"
   Serial #: 884 141
   Released: 1985
   7-inch vinyl 45: $3
   With picture sleeve: $5
   Promotional copy with picture
      sleeve: $7
"Beth"/"Hard Luck Woman"
   (Polygram reissue)
   Serial #: 814 303–7
   Released: 1986
   7-inch vinyl 45: $4
   No picture sleeve
   No promotional copies
"I Was Made for Lovin' You"/
"Rock and Roll All Nite"
   (Polygram reissue)
   Serial #: 814 304–7
   Released: 1986?
   7-inch vinyl 45: $4
   No picture sleeve
   No promotional copies
"Crazy Crazy Nights"/
"No, No, No"
   Serial #: 888 796
   Released: 1987
   7-inch vinyl 45: $3
   With picture sleeve: $5
   Promotional copy with picture
      sleeve: $7
"Reason to Live"/"Thief in the Night"
   Serial #: 870 022
   Released: 1987
   7-inch vinyl 45: $3
   With picture sleeve: $5
   Promotional copy with picture
      sleeve: $7
"Turn on the Night"/
"Hell or High Water"
   Serial #: 870 215
   Released: 1987
   7-inch vinyl 45: $3

With picture sleeve: $5
Promotional copy with picture
   sleeve: $7
"Beth"/"Hard Luck Woman"
   ("Timepieces" series reissue)
   Serial #: 814 303–7
   Released: 1988
   7-inch vinyl 45: $4
   No picture sleeve
   No promotional copies
"I Was Made for Lovin' You"/
"Rock and Roll All Nite"
   ("Timepieces" series reissue)
   Serial #: 814 304–7
   Released: 1988
   7-inch vinyl 45: $4
   No picture sleeve
   No promotional copies
"Let's Put the X in Sex"/
"Calling Dr. Love"
   Serial #: 872 246
   Released: 1988
   7-inch vinyl 45: $3
   With picture sleeve: $5
   Promotional copy with picture
      sleeve: $7
"Hide Your Heart"/"Betrayed"
   Serial #: 876 146
   Released: 1989
   7-inch vinyl 45: $3
   No picture sleeve
   Promotional copy: $6
"Forever"/
"The Street Giveth and the Street
Taketh Away"
   Serial #: 876 176
   Released: 1989
   7-inch vinyl 45: $3
   No picture sleeve
   Promotional copy: $6
"Forever" was the last single released
   on vinyl in the United States.

FOREIGN 45s

The following are lists of foreign 45s and 7-inch EPs, separated by country. Each list is set up chronologically. The lists are by no means complete, but they will give you an idea of the value of 45s from these countries. In some cases, we have listed a country and an approximate value but have not listed any specific singles. For 45s from countries not listed, assume that the prices are similar to those of the nearest listed country. If you have a foreign 45 that should have a picture sleeve but doesn't, its value is reduced dramatically, and it is probably worth about $2–3.

AUSTRIA

An Austrian 45, with a picture sleeve, is generally worth about $20–25 if it was released before KISS removed the makeup, or $15–20 if the 45 was released after the makeup came off. Some, although not most, Austrian 45s have the German KISS logo on them, rather than the standard KISS logo. Here is a partial list of 45s from Austria, with descriptions of the picture sleeves, and the values of the 45s (assuming mint condition, with picture sleeve):

"A World Without Heroes"—Sleeve shows band in *The Elder* outfits, with red logo. $25
"I"—Sleeve shows a black-and-white photo of band's faces, with a bright pink logo and the word "I" also in pink. $25

AUSTRALIA

An Australian 45, with a picture sleeve, is generally worth about $20–25 if it was released before KISS removed the makeup, or $17–19 if the 45 was released after the makeup came off.

CANADA

A Canadian 45, with a picture sleeve, is generally worth about $7–10 if it was released before KISS removed the makeup, or $5–7 if the 45 was released after the makeup came off. Although the singles released in Canada are probably the same as those released in the U.S., and their values are close to the same, we have listed a few here. Descriptions of the picture sleeves (where applicable), and the values of the 45s (assuming mint condition, with picture sleeve where applicable) are included:

"New York Groove"/"Snowblind", Ace—(1 of 4; Paul's is "Hold Me, Touch Me," Gene's is "Radioactive," and Peter's is "Don't You Let Me Down"); no picture sleeves (these came in standard Casablanca sleeves); Serial #NB941 (Casablanca Records and Filmworks). $7 each, $30 set of 4
"Lick It Up"/"Not for the Innocent"—Front shows color photo of band (GS/VV/EC/PS) without makeup; back has black-and-white band photo (also without makeup), with pink background and blue KISS logo; Serial #MS76206 (Mercury/Polygram Records). $10
"Crazy Crazy Nights"/"No No No"—No picture sleeve (these came in standard Canadian Polygram sleeves, white with red Polygram logo and Polygram's address in English on one side, in French on the other); Serial #MS76258. $7
"Reason to Live"/"Thief in the Night"—No picture sleeve (these came in standard Canadian Polygram sleeves, white with red Polygram logo and Polygram's address in English on one side, in French on the other); Serial #MS76262. $7

ENGLAND (U.K.)

An English 45, with a picture sleeve, is generally worth about $15–20 if it was released before KISS removed the makeup, or $10–14 if the 45 was released after the makeup came off, or a few dollars higher if it came with a fold-out poster sleeve, as many later U.K. 45s did. The following is a partial list of 45s from England, with descriptions of the picture sleeves, and the values of the 45s (assuming mint condition, with picture sleeve):

"Nothin' to Lose"/"Love Theme from KISS"—No picture sleeve; Serial #CBX503 (Casablanca). $20

"Hard Luck Woman"/"Calling Dr. Love" and "Beth"—(1st British KISS single under Pye Records distribution); picture sleeve is a silver and white version of the *Rock and Roll Over* cover art; Serial #CAN102. $30

"New York Groove"/"Snowblind"—(1 of 4; Paul's is "Hold Me, Touch Me," Gene's is "Radioactive," and Peter's is "Don't You Let Me Down"); sleeves are cover art from that member's solo LP; standard black vinyl; Serial #CAN135 (EMI Pye Records). $15 each, $60 set of 4

Solo-LP 45s—Same as above, but on colored vinyl (Paul's on purple, Gene's on red, Ace's on blue, and Peter's on green), with "masks" of each member's face in his own 45. $30 each, $120 set of 4

"I Was Made for Lovin' You"/"Hard Times"—No picture sleeve; Serial #CAN152 (Pye Records/Casablanca Records and Filmworks label). $12

"2000 Man"/"I Was Made for Lovin' You" and "Sure Know Something"—Front shows color photo of band in *Dynasty* outfits posed against black background; Serial #NB1001. $15

"Killer"/"I Love It Loud"—Special white sleeve shows illustration of Gene sticking tongue out, and tongue is separate piece with a tab, so that when tab is pulled, tongue sticks out further and eyes roll down; Serial #KISS 003 EMI. $25

"Creatures of the Night"/"Rock and Roll All Nite" (live)—Picture sleeve is *Creatures of the Night* original cover art, but purple instead of blue; label is the photo from the "Loudest Band in the World" promotional poster for this LP; Serial #KISS 4 811 122–7 (EMI Music). $20

"Heaven's On Fire"/"Lonely Is the Hunter"—Sleeve has illustration of fiery meteor streaking through space; silver Vertigo label; Serial #VER12 880 205–7 (Vertigo Records). $20

"Crazy Crazy Nights"/"No No No"—Limited edition poster bag; picture sleeve is *Crazy Nights* cover art, but "poster bag" which folds around sleeve has individual shots on one side, and the picture from the cover of the *KISS eXposed* videotape on the other; Serial #KISS P 7 888 796–7. $25

"Reason to Live"/"Thief in the Night"—Sleeve shows posed shot of band; this 45 came with a small, rectangular (3-by-4-inch) black patch with a gold-glitter KISS logo; Serial #KISS 8 870 022–7. $15 with patch, $10 without patch

"Turn On the Night"/"Hell Or High Water"—Limited edition poster bag; sleeve showed four individual head-and-shoulder shots of the band members; "poster bag" had individual live shots on one side, and many different pictures on the other side (including the ones on the sleeve); Serial #KISS P9 870 660–7. $25

"Hide Your Heart"/"Betrayed"—Sleeve photo is the same as the one from the *Hot in the Shade* promotional poster (band in front of beige wall, EC/GS/PS/BK); Serial #Vertigo 876 146–7 UK KISS 10. $12

"Hide Your Heart"/"Betrayed"—Same as above, but on red vinyl. $15

"Forever" (remix)/"The Street Giveth, the Street Taketh Away"—Sleeve photo is the *Hot in the Shade* back cover photo, with a yellow logo and the "postmark" with little KISS logos in it; this 45 came with a round red patch with a black

Some foreign picture-sleeve 45s. Top row (l. to r.): "Rock and Roll All Nite," Japan; "Hard Luck Woman," U.K.; "Calling Dr. Love," France. 2nd row: "Christine Sixteen," Japan; "I Was Made for Lovin' You," Germany; "I Was Made for Lovin' You," France. 3rd row: "Shandi," Mexico; "Talk to Me," Spain; "Killer," U.K. 4th row: "I'm a Legend Tonight," Japan; "Hide Your Heart," red vinyl, U.K.; and "Let's Put the X in Sex," U.K.

KISS logo and "Forever" in white; Serial #Vertigo KISS 11 876 716–7. $15
with patch; $10 without patch

"God Gave Rock and Roll to You II" (edit) by KISS/"Junior's Gone Wild" by King's
X—(both songs are from the *Bill and Ted's Bogus Journey* movie soundtrack);
sleeve photo is Bill and Ted pressing their faces against a pane of glass, with
the "Death" character behind them; Serial #A8696 (East/West Records). $10

FRANCE

A French 45, with a picture sleeve, is generally worth about
$12–17 if it was released before KISS removed the makeup, or
$10–14 if the 45 was released after the makeup came off. The
following is a partial list of 45s from France, with descriptions of
the picture sleeves, and the values of the 45s (assuming mint
condition, with picture sleeve):

"Calling Dr. Love"/"Take Me"—Front has *Destroyer* cover art; back has song titles;
Serial #140 226. $17

"I Was Made for Lovin' You"/"Hard Times"—Front has 4 individual LVG-era posed
photos; back has song titles; song credit for "Hard Times" lists Ace as
"H. Frehley"; Serial #1182. $17

"I Was Made for Lovin' You"/"Hard Times"—Front has 4 individual *Love Gun*–era
posed photos (same as above) and says "Disco Rock" above Ace's picture;
back has song titles and *Dynasty* cover art; song credit for "Hard Times" lists
Ace as "H. Frehley"; Serial #1182. $20

"Dirty Livin'"/"Sure Know Something"—Front has red logo and band photo in
Dynasty outfits; back has song titles and *Dynasty* cover art; Serial #1226. $17

"Magic Touch"/"Save Your Love"—Front shows posed shot of band in *Dynasty*
outfits, with instruments; back has song titles and *Dynasty* cover art; Serial
#101259. $15

"I"/"The Oath"—Front shows posed photo of band (with Eric Carr) in *The Elder*
outfits (from cover of *Killers* LP); Serial #6000 717. $17

GERMANY

Most German 45s have the German KISS logo, not the standard KISS logo. A German 45, with a picture sleeve, is generally
worth about $15–20 if it was released before KISS removed the
makeup, or $12–15 if the 45 was released after the makeup came

off. The following is a partial list of 45s from Germany, with descriptions of the picture sleeves, and the values of the 45s (assuming mint condition, with picture sleeve):

"Hold Me, Touch Me"/"Goodbye"—Front of sleeve is Paul's solo LP cover art; back shows all 4 solo LP covers (this is one of 4 45s, 1 from each member's solo LP; they are all worth the same amount); Serial #BF18636 (Bellaphon Records). $15 each, $60 set of 4

"I Was Made for Lovin' You"/"Hard Times"—Front shows posed photo of band in *Destroyer* outfits and a *standard* KISS logo; back has all the LPs up to *Double Platinum*, with a space for *Dynasty* that says "Dynasty/Neu" (new); Serial #BF1667 (Bellaphon Records). $20

"I Was Made for Lovin' You"/"Hard Times"—Front shows *Dynasty* cover art and red German logo; Serial #6175 014 (Phonogram Records). $20

"Dirty Livin'"/"Sure Know Something"—Front is *Dynasty* cover art; Serial #BF18684 (Bellaphon Records). $20

"Talk to Me"/"Naked City"—Front has red German logo and backward posed photo of band in *Dynasty* outfits (with Peter); back has German *Unmasked* tour dates; Serial #6000 463 (Phonogram Records). $18

"I"/"The Oath"—Front has red German logo and *The Elder* cover art and small photo of band in *The Elder* outfits under the logo; back is black with logo and song titles in white; Serial #6000 717 (Phonogram Records). $20

"All Hell's Breaking Loose"/"Gimme More"—Front has backward photo of band without makeup and black German KISS logo; Serial #818 108–7Q (Phonogram Records). $15

"Heaven's on Fire"/"Lonely Is the Hunter"—Front has red German logo and photo of Mark St. John, Paul, Eric Carr, and Gene against black background; back has *Animalize* cover art and song titles; Serial #880 205–7Q (Phonogram Records). $15

"(You Make Me) Rock Hard"/"Deuce"—Front shows gray, rocky surface with silver standard KISS logo outlined in blue and black, with song title underneath; back has song titles and *Smashes, Thrashes and Hits* cover art; Serial #874 052–7 (Phonogram/Vertigo Records). $15

HOLLAND (THE NETHERLANDS)

A Dutch 45, with a picture sleeve, is generally worth about $15–17 if it was released before KISS removed the makeup, or $12–15 if the 45 was released after the makeup came off. The following is a partial list of 45s from Holland, with descriptions of the picture sleeves, and the values of the 45s (assuming mint condition, with picture sleeve):

"Shandi"/"She's So European"—Front of picture sleeve has posed *Dynasty* shot; back shows *Unmasked* cover art; Serial #6000 436. $15

"Is That You?"/"Two Sides of the Coin"—Front has big yellow logo and small black-and-white posed picture of band onstage (with Eric); back is black-and-white picture of *Unmasked* cover art; Serial #6000 514. $15

"Lick It Up"/"Not for the Innocent"—Front of sleeve shows *Lick It Up* cover art; back shows song titles and small LP cover; Serial #814 498-7. $15

"Heaven's On Fire"/"Lonely Is the Hunter"—Front has illustration of fiery meteor streaking through space; back shows *Animalize* cover art and song titles; Serial #880–205-7. $12

"Let's Put the X in Sex"/"Calling Dr. Love"—Front has large gray X over blue cloth with the song title in red letters; back shows same X with small photos of each member; Serial #872 246-7. $12

ITALY

An Italian 45, with a picture sleeve, is generally worth about $12–15 if it was released before KISS removed the makeup, or $10–12 if the 45 was released after the makeup came off. The following is a partial list of 45s from Italy, with descriptions of the picture sleeves, and the values of the 45s (assuming mint condition, with picture sleeve):

"Christine Sixteen"/"Shock Me"—Both sides of sleeves show *Love Gun* cover art; Serial #CA504 (CA stands for Casablanca Records). $12

"Shout It Out Loud" (live)/"Nothin' to Lose" (live)—Both sides show live photo of band in *Destroyer* outfits; Serial #CA508. $14

"Hold Me, Touch Me"/"Goodbye", Paul—1 of 4 solo-LP singles (Gene's is "Radioactive," Serial #CA523; Peter's is "Don't You Let Me Down," Serial #CA521; Ace's is "New York Groove); each single has its own solo-LP cover art on both sides of sleeve, along with song titles; Serial #CA522 (Paul's). $14 each, $56 set of 4

"I Was Made for Lovin' You"/"Hard Times"—*Dynasty* cover art on both sides of sleeve; Serial #CA527. $14

"Shandi"/"She's So European"—*Unmasked* cover art on both sides of sleeve; Serial #CA539. $14

JAPAN

A Japanese 45 is generally worth about $25–30 if it was released before KISS removed the makeup, or $20–25 if the 45 was released after the makeup came off. Japanese 45s, rather than having actual picture sleeves, came with a plain sleeve and a 7-inch square paper sheet with a picture on it. The following is a partial list of 45s from Japan, with descriptions of the paper sheets, and the values of the 45s (assuming mint condition, with plain paper sleeve and picture sheet):

"Rock and Roll All Nite"/"Room Service"—*Dressed to Kill* cover art; Serial #JET2318. $30

"C'mon and Love Me"/"Getaway"—1974 photo of GS/PC/PS/AF; Serial #JET2335. $30

"Shout It Out Loud"/"Sweet Pain"—Live shot from 1975, Gene and Ace at mike, singing; Serial #VIP2408. $30

"Detroit Rock City"/"Beth"—Live shot from 1975, Gene and Ace at mike, singing (different from above); Serial #VIP2464. $25

"Calling Dr. Love"/"Take Me"—KISS logo with live shot of each member in each letter of the logo. $25

"Christine Sixteen"/"Shock Me"—*Love Gun* cover art; Serial #VIP2546. $25

"Love Gun"/"Hooligan"—1977 shot of band on Plexiglas cubes. $25

"Shout It Out Loud" (Alive II version)/"Nothin' to Lose" (Alive II version)—Live 1977 stage shot, taken during "Black Diamond"; Serial #VIP2584. $25

"I Was Made for Lovin' You"/"Hard Times"—*Dynasty* cover art, with logo on both sides of picture; Serial #VIP2752. $25

"Shandi"/"She's So European"—Individual shots of Gene, Ace, Paul, and Peter, with logo in center; Serial #Polystar 6S–6. $25

"Tomorrow"/"Naked City"—Posed shot from Palladium (with Eric Carr); Serial #Polystar 6S–14. $25

"Talk to Me"/"Easy As It Seems"—Live concert shot at Palladium; Serial #Polystar 7S–33. $25

"The Oath"/"Escape from the Island"—Individual shots of GS/PS/AF/EC in *Elder* outfits; Serial #Polystar 7S–54. $25

"I'm a Legend Tonight"/"Love Gun"—Small photos of each member (*The Elder* era), with "rising sun" motif behind them; Serial #Polystar 7S–70. $25

"I Love It Loud"/"Killer"—*Creatures of the Night* original cover art; Serial #Polystar 7S–78. $25

"Lick It Up"/"Not for the Innocent"—Individual shots of each member (GS/PS/EC/VV) in makeup; Serial #Polystar 7S–99. $25

"Heaven's On Fire"/"Lonely Is the Hunter"—Photo from back of *Lick It Up* cover; Serial #Polystar 7SA-124. $20

"Thrills in the Night"/"Murder in High Heels"—Studio photo of Gene, Eric Carr, Paul, and Mark St. John; Serial #Polystar 7SA-128. $20

"Tears Are Falling"/"Any Way You Slice It"—Posed group shot of Eric Carr, Gene, Paul, and Bruce Kulick; Serial #DO7R-2003. $20

MEXICO

A Mexican 45, with a picture sleeve, is generally worth about $16–18 if it was released before KISS removed the makeup, or $12–15 if the 45 was released after the makeup came off. All of the Mexican 45s we have seen are EPs, or extended-play 45s; that is, they have more than two songs on them (in this case, four songs on each 45). The following is a partial list of 45s from Mexico, with descriptions of the picture sleeves, and the values of the 45s (assuming mint condition, with picture sleeve):

"Strutter '78" and "Let Me Go, Rock and Roll"/"Love Gun" and "Beth"—Front of sleeve shows posed *Love Gun*–era shot with black border, with "Presumido 78" in red letters (Spanish for "Strutter '78"); Serial #2453. $18

"Radioactive" and "Hold Me, Touch Me"/"New York Groove" and "Don't You Let Me Down"—Sleeve shows live shots of each member; Serial #2463. $18

"I Was Made for Lovin' You" and "Nothin' to Lose"/"Let Me Go, Rock and Roll" and "Detroit Rock City"—*Dynasty* cover art; Serial #2466. $17

"Shandi" and "Mr. Make Believe"/"Firehouse" and "Let Me Go, Rock and Roll"—KISS logo and illustrated panel (from LP cover) of band removing masks; Serial #2472. $18

"Tomorrow" and "Sure Know Something"/"Christine Sixteen" and "She"—Front of picture sleeve has shots of each member (PS/GS/AF/PC) in *Dynasty* outfits; back shows posed band shot with Eric Carr; Serial #2475. $18

SPAIN

A Spanish 45, with a picture sleeve, is generally worth about $12–15 if it was released before KISS removed the makeup, or $10–12 if the 45 was released after the makeup came off. *45s from Portugal would have the same value as Spanish 45s.* The following is a partial list of 45s from Spain, with descriptions of

the picture sleeves, and the values of the 45s (assuming mint
condition, with picture sleeve):

"I Was Made for Lovin' You"/"Hard Times"—Both sides of sleeve are black with
    a KISS logo and "I Was Made for Lovin' You" in white; Serial #6175 014.
    $12
"Talk to Me"/"Naked City"—Front of sleeve shows posed shot of band in *Dynasty*
    outfits; back has *Unmasked* cover art; Serial #6000 463. $15
"Lick It Up"/"Not for the Innocent"—Front is *Lick It Up* cover art; back is black with
    white lettering; Serial #814 498–7. $12

U.S. 12-INCH SINGLES

"I Was Made for Lovin' You"/"Charisma"—Beige Casablanca Records and Filmworks cover with label hole. $8–10

U.S. 12-INCH PROMOTIONAL SINGLES

"I Was Made for Lovin' You"—Special one-sided single; Casablanca cover with
label hole. $10–12
"Lick It Up" b/w same—White cover with "KISS—Lick It Up—from the Forthcoming
Mercury Album of the Same Name" written in black and gray. $8–10
"All Hell's Breaking Loose" b/w same—Plain white cover with label hole. $8–10
"Heaven's On Fire" b/w same—White cover with "KISS—Heaven's On Fire—from
the Forthcoming Mercury Album Animalize" written in black. $8–10
"Thrills in the Night" b/w same—Plain white cover with label hole. $8–10
"Tears Are Falling" b/w same—Beige "ruler" cover, says "12 inch." $8–10
"Uh! All Night" b/w same—Green marbled "ruler" cover, says "12 inch." $8–10
"Crazy Crazy Nights" b/w same—Plain white cover with label hole. $8–10
"Reason to Live" b/w same—White cover with label hole, says "Polygram Rocks
Radio" in black. $8–10
"Turn On the Night" b/w same—White cover with label hole, says "Polygram
Rocks Radio" in black. $8–10
"Let's Put the X in Sex"—There are 4 different versions of the song on the 12-inch
promotional single. $20–25

U.S. PROMOTIONAL EPs

EP stands for extended play, as opposed to an LP (long
play). The term was created to describe 12-inch (or sometimes
10-inch) records that had more songs than a single but fewer than
an album. The term "sampler" refers to an EP that contains
sample songs from a particular album. These samplers made it

easier for radio stations to know which songs were considered by the record company to be appropriate for radio.

Destroyer Promo Sampler: White cover with "A Special KISS Album for Their Summer Tour Featuring Cuts for All Formats" written in large black letters. A black-and-white "U.S. Tour '76" photo of band is printed on the label of the album.
> Side One: "Beth"/"Do You Love Me"
> Side Two: "Flaming Youth"/"Detroit Rock City"
> Approximate Value: $35–40

Rock and Roll Over Promo Sampler: Black-and-white version of *Rock and Roll Over* cover with "Special Edition for Radio Station Airplay Only" written in top right corner.
> Side One: "I Want You"/"Hard Luck Woman"
> Side Two: "Take Me"/"Baby Driver"/"Love 'Em and Leave 'Em"
> Approximate Value: $35–40

A Taste of Platinum (*Double Platinum* Promo Sampler): Silver cover with label hole, with "KISS—a Taste of Platinum" in red letters.
> Side One: "Strutter '78"/"Do You Love Me"
> Side Two: "Love Gun"/"Firehouse"
> Approximate Value: $20–25

Solo Album Sampler: Black cover with label hole, with "Peter Criss—Ace Frehley—Gene Simmons—Paul Stanley—Assembled Especially for Radio from the KISS Albums" written in white.
> Side One: "Don't You Let Me Down"/"You Matter to Me"/"New York
>   Groove"/"Fractured Mirror"
> Side Two: "See You Tonite"/"Radioactive"/"Hold Me, Touch Me"/
>   "Take Me Away (Together As One)"
> Approximate Value: $20–25

First KISS, Last Licks (*Hot in the Shade* Promo Sampler with 4 older cuts): Color cover; top 1/3 of front cover shows Paul, Gene, Ace, and Peter (with makeup) on motorcycles; bottom 2/3 of front cover shows Eric, Gene, Paul, and Bruce (no makeup) blindfolded, standing up against a wall. A red circle next to Bruce has the words "Limited Collectors Edition—Includes Unreleased Songs" in red, and beneath it are the words "For Promotional Use Only—Not for Sale." The back cover has Paul's and Gene's handwritten synopses of the songs and how they were written. The labels on the record are fuzzy shots of Gene (Side One) and Paul (Side Two) in makeup, from the cover of *Hotter Than Hell*. Polygram released only 800 of these EPs, most copies shipped to record stores.
> Side One: "Love's a Slap in the Face"/"Betrayed"/"Prisoner of Love"/
>   "The Street Giveth, the Street Taketh Away"
> Side Two: "Nowhere to Run"/"Partners in Crime" (remixed)/"Deuce"
>   (demo version)/"Strutter" (demo version)
> Approximate Value: $40–50

U.S. promo samplers: *Destroyer* promo sampler ("A Special KISS Album for Their Summer Tour . . ."); *Rock and Roll Over* promo sampler; *Double Platinum* promo sampler ("A Taste Of Platinum"); Solo-LPs promo sampler; and *First KISS, Last Licks.*

FOREIGN 12-INCH SINGLES AND EPs

Use the following chart to determine the value of an import 12-inch single or EP by adding the amount shown to the preceding listed values.

All records are assumed to be in EX to mint condition. Value is reduced if condition is less than excellent.

It cannot be assumed that 12-inch singles were released in all of the countries listed, but these are countries that released KISS albums. If the record is an EP (that is, there are more than three songs but it is not a full album), $4–5 should be added to the value. Also add an additional $3–4 if the record is promotional.

	┌─Add this amount to U.S. value─┐	
	Without	**With**
Country	**Picture Sleeve**	**Picture Sleeve**
Argentina	$5	$12
Australia	$5	$10
Brazil	$5	$10
Canada	$3	$6
France	$5	$10
Great Britain	$4	$8
Greece	$5	$10
Italy	$5	$10
Israel	$10	$18
Japan	xx	$15
Mexico	$5	$10
The Netherlands	$4	$8
The Philippines	$5	$10
Portugal	$5	$10
Saudi Arabia	$8	$15
Spain	$5	$10
Taiwan	$8	$15
West Germany	$4	$8

CDs AND LASERDISCS

CDs

Because CDs were manufactured outside the United States before there was a consumer demand for them in America, the first CDs sold in the United States were made in West Germany, but specifically for sale in the U.S. Therefore, a CD that says, "Made in West Germany" isn't necessarily an import. If the CD booklet has the American KISS logo, it was a CD made to be sold in the U.S. If the booklet has the German KISS logo, it was made to be sold in Germany. So for our purposes, "U.S. CDs" will cover not only those CDs manufactured in the United States, but also those pressed in Europe specifically for release in America. Listed values assume mint condition, and titles marked with an asterisk were released as "Super Savers" or "bargain titles," meaning that their original CD retail price was only about $10.

U.S. CDs

Title	Value	Title	Value
KISS	$12	Dynasty	$12
Hotter Than Hell	$12	Unmasked	$12
Dressed to Kill	$12	The Elder*	$10
Alive!	$17 (double)	Creatures of the	(2nd cover)
Destroyer	$12	Night	$12
Rock and Roll Over	$12	Animalize	$12
Love Gun	$12	Asylum	$12
Alive II	$17 (double)	Crazy Nights	$12
Double Platinum	$12 (single)	Smashes, Thrashes	
Paul Stanley*	$10	and Hits	$12
Gene Simmons*	$10	Hot in the Shade	$12
Ace Frehley*	$10	Revenge	$12
Peter Criss*	$10		

There was also a 4-CD package called "First KISS" released in 1990, but it was just the first 4 studio albums (KISS, Hotter Than Hell, Dressed to Kill, and Destroyer) in a clear plastic package. There was no booklet or special packaging that would make it valuable; it is worth only the value of the 4 CDs.

67

The KISS catalog: KISS's 24 albums, on CD

U.S. CD SINGLES

Title	Size	Packaging	Value
"Let's Put the X in Sex"	3 inches	Cardboard sleeve	$12
"Hide Your Heart"	5 inches	Cardboard, picture CD	$8

U.S. PROMOTIONAL CD SINGLES

Title	Size	Packaging	Value
"Crazy Crazy Nights"	5 inches	Jewel box with cover sheet	$15
"Let's Put the X in Sex"	5 inches	Cardboard sleeve	$10
"Hide Your Heart"	5 inches	Jewel box, picture CD	$10
"Forever"	5 inches	Jewel box, picture CD	$12
"Forever" with "postcard"	5 inches	Same as above but with card	$15
"Rise to It"	5 inches	Jewel box with booklet, picture CD	$12
"God Gave Rock and Roll To You"	5 inches	Jewel box	$10
"God Gave Rock and Roll To You"	5 inches	Jewel box, picture CD ("Bill and Ted" logo)	$12
"Unholy" plus 3 tracks	5 inches	Jewel box with cover sheet	$18
"Domino"	5 inches	Cardboard sleeve	$12
"I Just Wanna"	5 inches	Jewel box	$10

FOREIGN CDs

Canada/Europe: $15 per single CD, $25 per double
Japan: $25 per single CD, $35 per double
Other Countries: $20 per single CD, $30 per double
Add $2–4 to these prices if the CD is promotional.

FOREIGN CD SINGLES

Within the values listed, the nicer the packaging of a CD, or the more tracks included, the higher the value. For example, a standard U.K. CD single would be worth $12, but a 4-song U.K. CD single with a fold-out poster booklet would be worth $20.

Canada/Europe: $12–20
Japan: $18–25
Other Countries: $15–20
Add $3–5 if the CD single is promotional.

CD singles, regular and promotional

LASERDISCS

Title	Size	Value
Animalize Live and Uncensored	12 inches	$25
Crazy Nights (3 videos)	8 inches	$15
KISS eXposed	12 inches	$25
KISS Meets the Phantom of the Park	12 inches	$25
Xtreme Close-Up	12 inches	$25

CDVs (COMPACT DISC VIDEOS)

CDVs, or compact disc videos, are 5-inch laserdiscs that contain one music video and several music-only tracks. The audio and video can be played on a laserdisc player, or the audio alone can be played on a standard CD player. The discs themselves, rather than being the silver color of a standard CD, are gold.

U.S. CDVs

Tears Are Falling CDV; also includes "Any Way You Slice It," "Who Wants to Be Lonely," and "Secretly Cruel" audio tracks. Cover sheet of jewel box is *Asylum* cover art. $15–18

Crazy Crazy Nights CDV; includes 3 other tracks. Cover sheet is *Crazy Nights* cover art. $15–18

Turn On the Night CDV; also includes "Hell Or High Water," "I'll Fight Hell to Hold You," and "When Your Walls Come Down" audio tracks. Cover sheet of jewel box shows the same 4 photos (1 each of PS, GS, EC, BK) that were used on the picture sleeve of the "Turn on the Night" U.S. 45. $15–18

Let's Put the X in Sex CDV; also includes "Rock and Roll All Nite" (spelled "Night" on this CDV, as on the *Smashes* CD), "Beth" (the Eric Carr version), and "Love Gun" audio tracks. Cover sheet of the jewel box is the *Smashes, Thrashes, and Hits* cover art. $15–18

FOREIGN CDVs

CDVs were also released outside the United States. Canadian or European CDVs would be worth about $3–4 more than U.S. CDVs, and Japanese CDVs would be worth $6–8 more.

CASSETTES, 8-TRACKS, AND REEL-TO-REEL TAPES

CASSETTES

Title	Value Orig./Later Press.	Title	Value Orig./Later Press.
KISS	$14/$8	(Music from) The Elder	2nd pr. (cover art on white background): $9
Hotter Than Hell	$12/$8		
Dressed to Kill	$12/$8		
Alive!	$15/$10 (double)		
Destroyer	$10/$7	Creatures of the Night	1st cover: $20
The Originals	$70/$60 complete	Creatures of the Night	2nd cover: $9
Rock and Roll Over	$10/$7	Lick It Up	$8*
Love Gun	$10/$7	Animalize	$8*
Alive II	$13/$10 (double)	Asylum	$8*
Double Platinum	$12/$9 (double)	Crazy Nights	$8*
Paul Stanley	$8/$6	Smashes, Thrashes, and Hits	$8*
Gene Simmons	$8/$6		
Ace Frehley	$8/$6		
Peter Criss	$8/$6	Hot in the Shade	$8*
Dynasty	$8/$6	Revenge	$8*
Unmasked	$8/$6		
The Elder	1st pr. (cover art on black background): $16		

* = No second pressing
All values assume mint condition.
"Universal presents Gimme KISS" promotional cassette: $18

For Canadian or European cassettes, add $3 per tape to the values above. For cassettes from other foreign countries, add $7 per tape.

CASSETTE SINGLES

A-side/B-side

"Beth"/"Hard Luck Woman"
("Timepieces" series reissue)
    Released: 1988
    Serial #: 814 303–4
    Value Sealed/Open: $4/$3
"Let's Put the X in Sex"/
"Calling Dr. Love"
    Released: 1988
    Serial #: 872 246–4
    Value Sealed/Open: $4/$3
"(You Make Me) Rock Hard"/
"Deuce"
    Released: 1988
    Serial #: 874 052–4
    Value Sealed/Open: $4/$3

A-side/B-side

"Hide Your Heart"/
"Betrayed"
    Released: 1989
    Serial #: 876 146–4
    Value Sealed/Open: $4/$3
"Forever"/
"The Street Giveth and the
Street Taketh Away"
    Released: 1989
    Serial #: 876 716–4
    Value Sealed/Open: $4/$3
"Rise to It"/"Silver Spoon"
    Released: 1989
    Serial #: 875 098–4
    Value Sealed/Open: $4/$3

For foreign cassette singles, add $2–4 to the above listed values.

Cassette singles

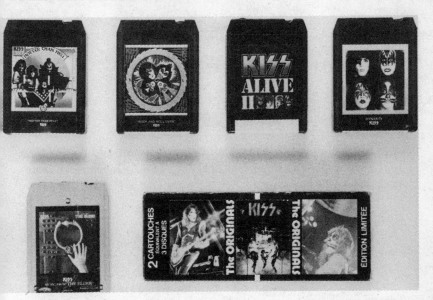

8-Track tapes (All of the ones pictured are from the U.S. except for *The Originals* double 8-Track set, which is from Canada.)

8-TRACK TAPES

U.S. 8-TRACKS

Title	Single/Double	Value
KISS	Single	$10
Hotter Than Hell	Single	$10
Dressed to Kill	Single	$10
Alive!	Double	$15
Destroyer	Single	$10
The Originals	Double	$70
Rock and Roll Over	Single	$10
Love Gun	Single	$10
Alive II	Double	$15
Double Platinum	Double	$15
Solo LPs	Single (sold separately)	$10 each
Dynasty	Single	$15
Unmasked	Single	$15

Title	Single/Double	Value
The Elder	Single	$30
Creatures of the Night (original cover only)	Single	$35

All values assume mint condition.

For Canadian or European 8-Track tapes, add $5 per tape to the values listed above. For 8-Tracks from other foreign countries, add $10 per tape.

REEL-TO-REEL TAPES

| Title | Value (assuming reel and box both mint) | |
	U.S.A.	Foreign
KISS	$45	$50
Hotter Than Hell	$40	$45
Dressed to Kill	$40	$45
Alive!	$55	$60
Destroyer	$40	$45
Rock and Roll Over	$40	$45
Love Gun	$40	$45
Alive II	$50	$55
Double Platinum	$50	$55
Solo LPs	$30 each	$35 each
Dynasty	$30	$35
Unmasked	$30	$35
Creatures of the Night (1st cover)	$35	$40
Any later LP	$25	$30

PICTURE DISCS

OFFICIAL U.S. PICTURE DISCS

Title	Year	Cover	Value
Paul Stanley (solo)	1978	Black with 12-inch hole	$40–50
Gene Simmons (solo)	1978	Black with 12-inch hole	$40–50
Ace Frehley (solo)	1978	Black with 12-inch hole	$40–50
Peter Criss (solo)	1978	Black with 12-inch hole	$40–50
Crazy Nights	1987	Clear plastic cover	$8–10
Smashes, Thrashes and Hits	1988	Same as LP but gatefold	$10–12

OFFICIAL FOREIGN PICTURE DISCS

ENGLAND (U.K.)

7-inch vinyl 45 picture disc—"A World Without Heroes"/"Mr. Blackwell." A-side photo is a group shot (GS/AF/PS/EC) in their *Elder* costumes, and a red KISS logo. B-side photo is the LP cover art. Serial #KISS P002. $15–20

7-inch vinyl 45 picture disc—"Lick It Up"/"Not for the Innocent." This picture disc is *shaped* like a tank (actual dimensions are 8.5 by 11 inches). A-side is an illustration of a tank with a silver KISS logo behind it, and the words "Lick It Up" in yellow in front of the tank. B-side photo is a non-makeup shot of GS/VV/EC/PS. Serial #KPIC 5(b) (814 498-7). $25–30

12-inch single picture disc (1987)—"Reason to Live," "Thief in the Night," "Who Wants to Be Lonely," and "Secretly Cruel." Serial #KISSP 812 870 058–1. $12–15

12-inch single picture disc (1987)—"Crazy Crazy Nights," "No No No," "Heaven's On Fire," and "Tears Are Falling." Serial #KISSP 712. $12–15

12-inch single picture disc (1987)—"Turn On the Night," "Hell Or High Water," "King of the Mountain," and "Any Way You Slice It." Serial #KISS SP 912 INT 870 661-1. $12–15

10-inch single picture disc (1989)—"Hide Your Heart," "Lick It Up," and "Heaven's On Fire." Serial #KISP 1010 INT 876 471–0. $12–15

HOLLAND (THE NETHERLANDS)

In 1987 and 1988, a company in Holland (The Netherlands) started producing picture discs of standard KISS albums. The albums were released in no particular order, and the company stopped printing them before they could release *Dressed to Kill*,

77

Set of picture disc LPs from the Netherlands

Some picture discs from the U.K.

Double Platinum, or either of the live albums. Each of these picture discs is numbered, and they are each worth about $35–40. (They may have been reproduced without numbers in the last couple of years. LPs that are not numbered are worth about $25–30.) These are the albums in this series:

KISS	*(Music from) The Elder*
Hotter Than Hell	*Killers*
Destroyer	*Creatures of the Night* (original cover)
Rock and Roll Over	*Lick It Up*
Love Gun	*Animalize*
Dynasty	*Asylum*
Unmasked	

JAPAN

Solo albums—*Gene Simmons, Paul Stanley, Ace Frehley, Peter Criss*. These were done as illustrated picture discs, and they are pretty hard to find. They are worth about $60 each, or $250 for the full set of 4.

BOOTLEG PICTURE DISCS

Because bootleg records are made in many different countries and in limited quantities, it is very difficult to put together a complete list. The following are some of the well-known bootleg concert and interview picture discs.

CONCERT PICTURE DISCS

KISS This—**A-side:** 1975 posed shot with cobwebs and half-naked woman; **B-side:** pornographic picture. Concert is 9/29/80; Rome, Italy. $30–35
KISS Still Love You—Double album. Picture is the same as the LP cover of the black vinyl issue of this bootleg (Gene, Vinnie, and Paul on the *Lick It Up* tank stage). Concert is 10/24/83; Leicester, England. $45–50

INTERVIEW PICTURE DISCS

Serial #MM1205—12-inch disc. **A-side:** makeup shot with *Alive!* costumes, red background; **B-side:** solid red with square concert photo (BK/GS/EC/PS) from *Animalize* tour. $12–15

Serial #BAK2026—12-inch disc. **A-side:** makeup shot with *Alive!* costumes, red background, Ace's eyes are closed; **B-side:** makeup shot of GS/PS/EC/AF with *Unmasked* costumes. $12–15

Serial #TT III B—12-inch disc. **A-side:** live shot of Gene from *Lick It Up* tour; **B-side:** live shot (GS/VV/PS) from *Lick It Up* tour. $12–15

(No Serial #)—12-inch disc. **A-side:** live shot of Paul from *Animalize* tour. Print says, "photos: Wayne Youngman. Interviewed 1981." **B-side:** live shot of Paul and Gene from *Animalize* tour. Print says, "KISS interview disc—limited edition." $12–15

Serial #CT1012—12-inch disc. **A-side:** live shot of GS/BK/PS from *Animalize* tour, and "KISS" written in silver; **B-side:** makeup shot of AF/PS/GS/PC in *Alive!* outfits posed with half-naked women. "KISS—The Chris Tetley Interview" is written in silver. The disc comes in a silver cover with 12-inch hole. $12–15

Serial #TTS1005—This picture disc came in two different 12-inch *shapes*, a bat or a sawblade. Both discs have the same photos and serial number. **A-side:** one band shot from 1976 with the words "KISS Then," and one backward *Animalize* photo (PS/BK/GS) with the words "And Now." **B-side:** same 1976 shot, only larger, with the words "Limited Edition Picture Disc." $12–15 (each)

An Interview With Gene Simmons and Paul Stanley (no Serial #)—Set of 4 color 7-inch picture discs. **Disc One:** A-side and B-side each show a different *Unmasked* close-up of Gene. **Disc Two:** the A-side shows a live *Creatures* group shot, and the B-side shows a *Creatures* shot of Gene. **Disc Three:** A-side shows a live *Creatures* shot of Vinnie Vincent, and the B-side shows a shot of Gene, just before he spits blood, also from the *Creatures* tour. **Disc Four:** the A-side shows a live *Lick It Up* tour shot of Eric Carr, and the B-side shows a live *Unmasked* shot of Gene. The same 17-minute October 1983 interview is on each disc. $10–12 each, $50 set of 4.

Serial #BAKPAK1002—Set of four 7-inch black-and-white picture discs in a clear plastic holder with a black-and-white cardboard panel at the top. All 4 B-sides have the same photo: a posed group shot (PS/GS/EC/AF) from the *Creatures* era. The A-sides are individual shots from the same photo session; Disc One is Gene, Disc Two is Eric Carr, Disc Three is Paul, and Disc Four is Ace. The interview continues from A-side to A-side, as each B-side contains the same interview segment as its corresponding B-side. The interview is with Gene, done just before the release of *Crazy Nights* in 1987. $25–30 (full set with holder)

KISS pinball machine
(Marcello Baca)

KISS dolls

(Karen Lesniewski)

KISS beach towel and toy guitar

(Karen Lesniewski)

KISS poster art set and notebooks

(Karen Lesniewski)

KISS garbage can,
record player, and backpack

(Karen Lesniewski)

KISS pen, ViewMaster reels, set of 6 pencils, and radio

(Karen Lesniewski)

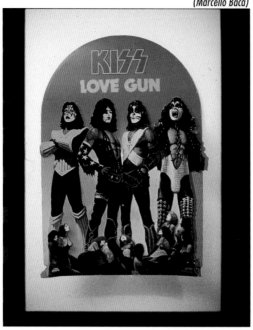

*L*ove *Gun* promotional cardboard standup

KISS "Flame" jacket, "Tank" jacket, "Universal presents Gimme KISS" promotional cassette, lunchbox, and thermos

K ISS "On Tour" game, Colorforms,
and Rub 'n' Play set

K ISS Halloween costumes

KISS jigsaw puzzles

KISS songbooks: *Destroyer, The Originals, Rock and Roll Over, Love Gun, Alive II, Double Platinum,* the solo albums, *Dynasty, Unmasked,* and *Crazy Nights*

Some KISS T-shirts from the makeup years

Some post-makeup KISS T-shirts

(Karen Lesniew

A Paul Stanley "Firehouse" hat, Eric Carr and Peter Criss drumsticks, and assorted KISS guitar picks

(Karen Lesniew

KISS remote control van, model van, and makeup kit

TEST PRESSINGS, COLORED VINYL, AND MISPRINTS

TEST PRESSINGS

Test pressings of vinyl albums are the 1st pressings made by the factory. Used to determine album quality, they are usually pressed onto black vinyl with a blank white label. Sometimes they're put into a blank white cardboard cover, but often they're put into a regular album cover. Because so few test pressings are made (only a handful per pressing plant per album), they are rather rare. If possible, when you buy a test pressing, ask the seller to play the first track for you (or you can hold it up and compare it to a regular copy of that album) so that you know that the album you're buying is really a test pressing of that LP, not a Duran Duran test pressing in a KISS sleeve! There are also test pressings of 45s, and they are also valuable collector's items. Approximate values are as follows:

U.S. LP TEST PRESSINGS: *(For foreign test pressings, add $5–10)*

Title	Value	Title	Value
KISS	$90	Ace Frehley	$60
Hotter Than Hell	$75	Peter Criss	$60
Dressed to Kill	$75	Dynasty	$60
Alive!	$90	Unmasked	$60
Destroyer	$75	The Elder	$70
The Originals	$110	Creatures of the Night	$70
Rock and Roll Over	$70	Lick It Up	$50
Love Gun	$70	Animalize	$50
Alive II	$80	Asylum	$50
Double Platinum	$75	Crazy Nights	$50
Paul Stanley	$60	Smashes, Thrashes and Hits	$50
Gene Simmons	$60	Hot in the Shade	$50

U.S. 45 TEST PRESSINGS: *(For foreign 45s, add $5)*

Years	Value
1974–1978	$20
1979–1982	$15
1983–1990	$12

COLORED VINYL

LPs

Country	Album	Color	Value	Notes
England	*KISS*	Opaque Red	$15–20	*Love Gun* label/ Pye
England	*Hotter Than Hell*	Opaque Red	$15–20	*Love Gun* label/ Pye
England	*Dressed to Kill*	Opaque Red	$15–20	*Love Gun* label/ Pye
England	*Alive!*	Opaque Red	$25–30	*Love Gun* label/ Pye
England	*Destroyer*	Opaque Red	$15–20	No *Love Gun* art on label/Pye
England	*Rock and Roll Over*	Opaque Red	$15–20	No *Love Gun* art/ Pye
England	*Love Gun*	Opaque Red	$15–20	*Love Gun* label/ Pye
England	*Alive II*	Opaque Red	$25–30	*Love Gun* label/ Pye
Germany	*Dynasty*	Opaque Red	$15–20	Casablanca Label

12-INCH SINGLES

Country	Title	Color	Value	Notes
Mexico	"I Was Made . . ."	Clear Red	$15–20	Casablanca Label
France	"I Was Made . . ."	Clear Red	$15–20	Dynasty Label
France	"I Was Made . . ."	Yellow	$15–20	Dynasty Label
England	"Unholy"	White	$15–20	With 3 other songs

45s

Country	Title	Color	Value	Notes
England	"Radioactive"	Opaque Red	$20	Came with mask
England	"Hold Me, Touch Me"	Purple	$20	Came with mask
England	"New York Groove"	Blue	$25	Came with mask
England	"Don't You Let Me Down"	Green	$20	Came with mask
England	"Hide Your Heart"	Red	$15	

BOOTLEG

Album	Number of LPs	Color	Concert Place/Date	Value
Fried Alive	1	"Tortoise"	Long Beach, CA, 1974	$50
KISS Destroys Anaheim	2	(Unknown)	Anaheim, CA, 8/20/76	$50
Simmons Meteor	1	Opaque Red	San Francisco, 1977	$25
Sneak Attack	2	Lavender (Marbled)	Los Angeles, 8/25/77	$50
Talk To Me	2	Clear Blue	Wembley, England, 9/9/80	$50
Unmasked	2	Opaque Red	Wembley, England, 9/9/80	$50
Love KISS from Hell	2	Opaque Red	France, 10/31/83	$45
Face Lift (Box set w/insert)	3	Opaque Red	Brussels, 11/12/83	$70
A Black Diamond	1	Blue	Lick It Up Demos	$22
Hall of Fame	1	Multicolor	Nashville, 1/11/84	$25
KISS My Ass	2	Clear Pink	Milwaukee, 12/30/84	$50
Framed	1	Opaque Red	1985 Interview w/Gene	$18

MISPRINTS

A misprint is a piece of printed matter (for our purposes, a record cover, label, or sleeve) that is printed incorrectly. Misprints range from the rare and unusual (such as the *Alive II* misprint, see page 84) to the very common (such as the *Love Gun*

misprint, see below). The KISS 1978 solo albums are the most
likely to be misprinted, and it's easy to see why . . . 4 albums on
the same label, with similar artwork and close serial numbers,
pressed at numerous pressing plants, and released on the exact
same day. The possibility of getting confused was tremendous.
What happened was that some solo albums were made that have
either no faces on the labels, or a face on 1 label but not the
other, or one person's label on another person's album! Other
misprints probably exist in addition to the ones listed below, but
these are some we have seen. All values assume VG/EX condition.

Love Gun Misprint: This is a very common misprint. The labels on the LP lists the
    songs in the wrong order, and Ace's name is spelled "Freeley" on the songwrit-
    ing credit "Shock Me." $6–8
Alive II Misprint: This misprint is very rare. The album cover lists the songs in the
    wrong order, and also lists 3 extra songs ("Take Me," "Hooligan," and "Do
    You Love Me") on the back. (The actual records, however, contain the usual
    songs in the usual order.) What is interesting about this misprint is that this song
    list (this order, with the 3 extra songs) is the actual song list done at the L.A.
    Forum when *Alive II* was recorded (except for "Hard Luck Woman" and
    "Tomorrow and Tonight" and the songs from Side Four). Apparently the origi-
    nal plan was to use the concert exactly as it was recorded, add "Hard Luck
    Woman" and "Tomorrow and Tonight," and then put the new studio songs on
    Side Four. No one knows for sure how many copies were printed with the
    original song list, but look for them, because they are quite valuable. $90–100
Solo LP Misprints: There are probably a large number of solo album misprints in
    existence. LPs with no faces on the labels (or a face on one side but not the
    other) are generally worth about $8–10. Albums with one member's label but
    another member's music on the record are worth $20–25. *All* Paul Stanley solo
    CDs released in the U.S. have "Wouldn't You Like to Know Me" listed as
    "Wouldn't You Like Me to Know," so they're not particularly valuable.
Double Platinum Misprint: There are copies of *Double Platinum* that, instead of
    having Paul, Gene, Ace, and Peter etched into the inside gatefold, have Paul,
    Gene, Paul, and Gene! This is a very rare misprint (we've only seen one), and
    is probably worth about $50.

THE BOOTLEG MUSIC

RECORDS

Album	Number of LPs	Show Date/ Tour	Place	Notes	Value
Blitz London	1	5/16/76, U.K. Destroyer	London	Japanese issue; starts with "Deuce"	$40
Lunchbox	1	5/16/76	London	Reissue of Blitz L.	$20
Fried Alive	1	5/31/76	Long Beach, CA	Tortoiseshell (Multicolor) vinyl	$50
Fried Alive	1	5/31/76	Long Beach, CA	Black vinyl original press.	$35
Light Years Ahead	1	5/31/76	Long Beach, CA	Reissue of Fried Alive (black vinyl)	$20
Stoned in Paris	1	5/22/76 French Destroyer	Olympia, Paris	B&W cover with green or red lettering	$20
Destroys Anaheim, Pts. 1 & 2	2	8/20/76	Anaheim, CA	Parts 1 and 2 were sold separately	$30 each part
Destroys Anaheim	2	8/20/76	Anaheim, CA	Colored vinyl reissue	$50
Mama We're All Crazee Now	1	4/1/77	Tokyo	1/2 of show	$30
Takes Tokyo	2	4/1/77	Tokyo	Full show	$35

cont.

Album	Number of LPs	Show Date/ Tour	Place	Notes	Value
Vintage KISS	1	4/2/77	Tokyo	Audio of HBO TV special	$15
Sneak Attack	2	8/25/77, *Love Gun* tour	Los Angeles	Black vinyl	$35
Sneak Attack	2	8/25/77	Los Angeles	Multicolored vinyl	$50
KISS Karton (box set)	3	5/16/76 & 8/25/77	London & Los Angeles	Contains *Blitz L.*, *Sneak Attack*, poster	$80
Simmons Meteor	1	9/77	San Francisco	Red vinyl LP with cool full-color cover	$25
KISS My Ass	1	8/25/77	Los Angeles		$30
KISS This	1	8/29/80	Rome	Picture disc with X-rated B-side picture	$30–35
Egos at Stake	1	9/9/80	Wembley, England	1/2 of show; released with several covers	$25 each
Egos at the Stake	2	9/9/80	Wembley, England	Full show; color cover with 4 photos	$35
Unmasked	2	9/9/80	Wembley, England	Full show; pressed on red vinyl	$50
Talk to Me	2	9/9/80	Wembley, England	Blue vinyl	$50
Live in Australia 1980	1	11/21/80	Sydney	Audio from the "Inner Sanctum" TV special	$25

Album	Number of LPs	Show Date/ Tour	Place	Notes	Value
Firehouse	2	11/18/80	Adelaide, Australia	12 of the 17 songs	$25
Rock and Roll	1	Nov. 15/ 18/21, 1980	Australia	Cuts from Melbourne/ Adelaide/Sydney	$30
Unmasked	2	1/15/83, *Creatures of the Night* tour	Ottowa	Cover has Paul without makeup	$30
10th Anni- versary Tour	3	3/27/83	Los Angeles	Very rare bootleg	$75
KISS Still Love You	2	10/24/83, *Creatures of the Night* tour	Leicester, England	Black vinyl	$30
KISS Still Love You	2	10/24/83, *Creatures of the Night* tour	Leicester, England	Full-color picture discs	$45– 50
Love KISS from Hell	2	10/31/83	Paris	Red vinyl	$45
Face Lift (box set)	3	11/13/83	Brussels	Box set with paper insert; black vinyl	$45
Face Lift (box set)	3	11/13/83	Brussels	Box set with paper insert; red vinyl	$70
The Tickler	1	11/18/83	Sweden	Gothenburg, Sweden	$25

cont.

Album	Number of LPs	Show Date/ Tour	Place	Notes	Value
A Black Diamond	1	1983	studio	*Lick It Up* demos; blue vinyl	$22
American Tour '84	1	1/11/84	Nashville	*King Biscuit Flour Hour* radio show	$20
Live Nashville	1	1/11/84	Nashville	Same as above	$20
Live In Boston	1	1/11/84	Nashville	Same as above	$20
Hall of Fame	1	1/11/84	Nashville	Same as above, but on multicolor vinyl	$25
Heavy Metal Holocaust	1	1/11/84	Nashville	Same as above, but with Judas Priest and Thin Lizzy tracks	$25
Hell Riders	1	1/11/84	Nashville	5 songs from show	$20
World Tour '84	3	1/27/84	Long Beach, CA		$40
Whites of Their Eyes	2	3/13/84, *Lick It Up* tour	Montreal	Black-and-white cover	$20
War Machine	2	3/13/84	Montreal	Reissue/color cover	$25
Beware of Imposters	2	10/11/84, *Animalize* tour	Ipswich, England		$25
Live at the Gaumont	2	10/11/84	Ipswich, England	Same show, different cover	$25

Album	Number of LPs	Show Date/ Tour	Place	Notes	Value
KISS Hit Wembley	1	10/14/84	Wembley, England		$15
They Only Come Out at Night	2	10/26/84	Stockholm	Black-and-white cover (original press.)	$25
They Only Come Out at Night	2	10/26/84	Stockholm	Deluxe issue with color cover and 12-page black-and-white booklet	$30
More Metallic Mayhem	1	10/27/84	Gothenburg, Sweden	Partial show	$20
Live Without a Net	2	10/27/84	Gothenburg, Sweden	Full show	$25
Jungle Fever	1	11/4/84	Zwolle, Holland	Part One	$20
Dressed to Kill	1	11/4/84	Zwolle, Holland	Part Two	$20
KISS Blows Your Head Off, Pt. 1	1	12/7/84	Ft. Wayne, IN	Part One	$20
KISS Blows Your Head Off, Pt. 2	1	12/7/84	Ft. Wayne, IN	Part Two	$20
KISS and Tell	2	12/8/84	Detroit	Audio of *Animalize Live Uncensored*	$25
Fits Like a Glove	2	12/8/84	Detroit	Not full show	$25

cont.

Album	Number of LPs	Show Date/ Tour	Place	Notes	Value
Barbarize	2	12/30/84	Milwaukee	Illustrated "warrior" on cover	$25
KISS My Ass	2	1/31/85	Houston	Black vinyl	$25
KISS My Ass	2	1/31/85	Houston	Pink vinyl	$50
Animalize	2	2/9/85	Oakland, CA		$30
KISSing The Pink	2	2/17/85	Long Beach, CA		$30
Framed	1	1985	interview	1985 interview with Gene, on red vinyl	$18
Walking Around the World	2	1/17/86	Chicago		$30
Asylum World Tour '86	2	2/11/86, *Asylum* tour	Los Angeles		$30
A Step Ahead	1	4/1/86	Allentown, PA		$15
Still Crazy	2	9/16/88	Sweden	Gothenburg, Sweden	$30
Starry Eyed	1	3/11/89	The Ritz, New York City	Paul Stanley 1989 solo tour concert	$15

CDs

The following are a few of the bootleg CDs available. There are many others, and their sound quality varies greatly from CD to CD.

Wicked Lester/KISS Demos—CD of Gene's and Paul's pre-KISS band, with KISS 1st-LP demos added; excellent sound quality; cover shows PS/GS/AF/PC holding candles and posing in white robes in "snow." $35–40

KISS: The Originals—This 3-CD set was a bootleg of *The Originals* that used actual copies of the *KISS, Hotter Than Hell,* and *Dressed to Kill* CDs, but with a bootlegged cover that looked like the cover of *The Originals.* When it first came out, many dealers tried to pass it off as an official release from Japan, but word soon got out that it was not official. $20–25

They Only Come Out at Night—Double CD of KISS's 10/26/84 show from Gothenburg, Sweden; 1980 live German shot on cover. $50–55

KISS Live in Hell—CD with 5 songs from Cleveland 3/29/75 and 5 songs taken from the *eXposed* video; cover shows 1982 group shot. $25–30

San Bernadino—CD of KISS's 2/20/85 show in San Bernadino, CA; cover is an illustration of PS/GS/AF/PC in cowboy hats. $25–30

Land of the Rising Sun—Double CD of KISS's 4/22/88 Tokyo concert (audio is taken from a vinyl LP, recorded during a Japanese TV special); cover picture is a 1988 shot of Paul and Gene. $50–55

A Crazy Night With KISS—Double CD of KISS's 6/17/90 concert in Middletown, NY; cover is a 1988 band shot. $50–55

KISS/Fifteen Years On—A *Crazy Nights*-era interview with Gene; the cover is a 1981 group shot with a red background, and the border is white; the CD is a picture disc with 4 separate shots of the band members from the same 1981 photo session. $15–20

KISS/The Conversation Disc Series—Snippets of many different interviews; the cover is a 1980 group shot with a yellow border; the CD is a picture disc with the same shot on the CD as on the cover. $15–20

<u>AUDIOTAPES (CASSETTES)</u>

Because audiotapes (cassettes) can be copied so easily, once a bootleg tape begins to be circulated, it is soon widely available. Therefore, no audiotape, even a "demo," is really "rare." In general, bootleg audiotapes go for about $6–8, with higher prices paid ($7–9) for tapes that use high-grade (metal) blanks or that have full-color inserts. These prices assume *at least* a full hour of material on the tape.

VIDEOTAPES

OFFICIAL U.S. VIDEOTAPES

KISS Meets the Phantom of the Park—KISS's 1978 movie, which was shown on television in the U.S. but was a theatrical release in Europe, was originally released on videotape in the U.S. in 1986 with a hard plastic case and a $59.95 price tag. It was re-released in 1989 with a cardboard sleeve and a $9.98 retail price. Value: 1st edition, $20; 2nd edition, $10 sealed

KISS: Animalize Live Uncensored—KISS's *Animalize* tour, live on video. Cardboard sleeve. The retail price is $24.95. Value: $20–25

Hot Licks Video: Bruce Kulick of KISS/Rock Master Class—This 1986 hour-long guitar lesson on videotape has Bruce explaining his technique and playing some of his KISS solos. Tapes in this series come in a hard case and retail for around $49.95. Value: $40–45

KISS eXposed—A hilarious and exciting compilation of interview segments, live clips, and videos (1975 to 1986). Cardboard sleeve. Retail price is $29.95. Value: $25–30

KISS: Crazy Nights—This video contains the 3 videos from the *Crazy Nights* LP: "Turn On the Night," "Reason to Live," and "Crazy Crazy Nights." Both "Reason to Live" and "Crazy Crazy Nights" are slightly different versions from those shown on MTV, and the footage at the beginning and end of the tape is cool. Cardboard sleeve. Retail price is $12.95. Value: $8–13

KISS: Xtreme Close-Up—This 1992 documentary was a more serious and informative follow-up to *KISS eXposed*. It chronicles the band's history and contains band footage from 1974 to 1992. Cardboard sleeve. Retail price is $19.95. Value: $20

U.S. PROMOTIONAL VIDEOTAPES

Promotional videotapes are sometimes released to TV and radio stations when a new video is made by the band. They are hard to find, and they usually consist of a plainly labeled videotape inside a black plastic case with the name of the band and video typed on a sticker, or in a white cardboard sleeve with an identifying sticker on it. In general, promotional KISS videos before 1984 (with makeup) are worth about $20–25, and promotional videos after 1984 (without makeup) are worth about $15–20.

KISS's official U.S. video catalog (*KISS Meets the Phantom, Animalize Live Uncensored, KISS eXposed, Crazy Nights,* and *X-Treme Close-Up*) and a promo video for the "Let's Put the X in Sex" video (white box with sticker)

IMPORTED AND "VARIOUS ARTIST" VIDEOTAPES

There are several "various artist" videotapes ("video magazines") that contain interviews with different bands, and KISS has appeared on several of them, including *Metalhead* and volumes 3 and 6 (and possibly others) of the *Hard & Heavy* video series. Because there is usually only 5 or 10 minutes of KISS on the videos, they are worth only about $10 each.

There are also imported videotapes that are mass-produced in other countries (but in VHS format for sale in the United States), and at least one of these tapes features KISS. It is called *The Interview Sessions*, and it is a collection of television interviews with KISS. Unfortunately, many of these interviews have been circulating for years among KISS video traders, sometimes in better quality than they are seen on this tape. Because of the low quality of some of the tape, and because the interviews are not particularly rare, it is only worth about $12–14.

BOOTLEG VIDEOTAPES

Bootleg videos are tapes not officially released by KISS. They are usually sold at record conventions or through the mail by private individuals. They include live concerts (both professionally shot and hand-held), interviews, and television appearances. A single tape usually consists of one concert or a compilation of interviews and TV clips, and most bootleg videos sell for $20–25. Sometimes video dealers claim that a tape is "rare" and they try to charge more for it—this is absurd. Once a video is distributed, it gets copied and resold by other dealers until the market is saturated. Therefore, *no bootleg videotape, regardless of content, is worth more than $25!* Also, the videotape should contain at least 75 minutes of material; most are 90 to 120 minutes. Beware of people selling 30 minutes of "rare" video for $35.

THE
MERCHANDISE

POSTERS, PHOTOS, AND POSTCARDS

POSTERS

There have been hundreds of officially released posters of KISS over the course of their 20-year (and counting!) history, as well as dozens of official promotional posters, and even some bootleg posters. It would be impossible to list every KISS poster ever made, but the list below contains 100 or so, along with their values. The 1st list contains promotional posters, both U.S. and foreign; the 2nd is non-promotional U.S. posters; the 3rd list is non-promotional foreign posters. A poster listed as from the U.S. could also have been used or sold outside the U.S., especially if the subject of the poster is an LP, used to advertise the CD and cassette as well. All posters are assumed to be approximately 2 by 3 feet unless otherwise noted. All values assume mint condition. (For album flats, see "Promotional Merchandise.")

PROMOTIONAL POSTERS

Key: Subject of Poster/Country of Origin/Description/Value

Double Platinum LP, U.S.—Black cardboard poster with silver KISS logos, "Double Platinum" in red, and photos of Gene, Paul, Peter, and Ace at the bottom. $50

Honda KISSmobile Motorcycle, U.S.—Red background, says, "Honda KISS-mobile" in black at top; shows Gene and Paul with motorcycle (KISS logos painted on various parts of the bike); bottom has radio station logo. $90–100

Dynasty LP, U.S.—"Return of KISS" and LP cover art, previous LPs at bottom. $25

Unmasked European tour, Germany—Shows *Dynasty* LP cover and red logo against silver background, and show date is June 16, 1980 (show never happened). $40

The Elder LP, U.S.—Photo of Eric Carr, Gene, Paul, and Ace, with pink smoke behind them; bottom says, "The New KISS album," and shows LP cover. $35

The Elder LP, U.S.—Clear plastic poster, 16 by 20 inches, with photo from LP cover/label (hand and door knocker). $50

Creatures of the Night LP, U.S.—Poster is mainly blue, with LP cover and "The Loudest Band in the World" at top; bottom is photo of Gene, Paul, Ace, and Eric Carr, in makeup, standing in a rocky area with fog at their feet; this poster was reprinted several years later. $15

Creatures of the Night LP, U.S.—LP cover art. $30

99

Honda KISSmobile poster (autographed) and 1980 fantasy poster.

Back of 1990 two-sided poster and *Revenge* promotional poster (U.S.)

Lick It Up European tour, Germany—LP cover art plus "Nov. 2, 1983, with special guest Helix." $15

Animalize LP, U.S.—Back cover photo from LP, with previous LPs at bottom. $20

Animalize Live Uncensored video, U.S.—Collage of live shots with woman's hand "ripping" through poster. $30

Animalize European tour, U.K.—Black-and-white poster with orange; shows logo at top and bottom and picture of Gene, Paul, Eric Carr, and Mark St. John, along with tour dates for the U.K. $40

Animalize European tour, Germany—Back cover photo from LP; says, "October 1984," with "Special Guest Bon Jovi." $15

Asylum LP, U.S.—2-foot-square poster of LP cover art; "On Mercury Records, Cassettes, and Compact Discs" at bottom. $15

KISS Meets the Phantom video, U.S.—17-by-22-inch poster made for the movie's original video release in 1986; light blue background with illustration of Peter Criss, Gene, and Abner Devereaux (a character from the movie); white print says, "Halloween the Way It Was Meant to Be . . . a Little Strange . . . and a Lot Of Fun." $25

Ludwig Drums, U.S.—Photo of Eric Carr sitting at a drum kit; background is black with black KISS logos. $20

Crazy Nights LP, U.S.—20-by-16-inch poster; black background with yellow KISS logo, and "Crazy Nights" in purple; says, "Coming Soon" at top, but that section of the poster is perforated for removal; poster would be 12 by 16 inches when that piece is removed. $10

Crazy Nights LP, U.S.—2-foot-square poster of LP cover art; "Available on Mercury Compact Discs, Chrome Cassettes, and Records" at bottom. $15

Crazy Nights LP/*KISS eXposed* video, U.S.—10.5-by-22-inch vertical poster; black background with "KISS/Crazy Nights/The Album" at top; picture of *KISS eXposed* cover in center; and "KISS eXposed/The Video" at bottom. $10

Crazy Nights European tour, U.K.—Black poster with white logo and photos of each band member, with tour dates. $12

Crazy Nights European tour, U.K.—40-by-60-inch poster shows LP cover art on blue background; "KISS/Crazy Nights" at top; bottom says, "Includes the hit single Crazy Crazy Nights/KISS eXposed/The Video/More videos, more women, more music than ever before." $25

Smashes, Thrashes and Hits LP, U.S.—20-by-16-inch poster; salmon-colored background, black KISS logo, and "Smashes, Thrashes and Hits" in white; says, "Coming Soon" at top, but that section of the poster is perforated for removal; poster would be 12 by 16 inches when that piece is removed. $10

Smashes, Thrashes, and Hits LP, U.S.—2-foot-square poster of LP cover art; "ON MERCURY COMPACT DISCS, CHROME CASSETTES AND LPS" at bottom. $12

Smashes, Thrashes, and Hits LP, U.S.—3-foot-square poster of LP cover art; "ON MERCURY COMPACT DISCS, CHROME CASSETTES AND LPS" at bottom. $20

Hot in the Shade LP, U.S.—Band photo (EC/GS/PS/BK) against a beige wall; LP cover and "postmark" at bottom. $15

Hot in the Shade LP, U.S.—Double-sided poster; front has giant picture of Sphinx with blue background; at top it says, "Hot in the Shade Tour/Rockin' America '90" in red, and at bottom is a KISS logo with one member in each letter; back says, "Have You Been KISSed Lately?" in pink and shows all of KISS's albums up to *Hot*, with the album title and serial number below each album (*Animalize* is misspelled "Animalze"). $20

Hot in the Shade LP, U.S.—12-by-20-inch poster is light blue and has dark blue KISS logo and *Hot in the Shade* "postmark"; below that it says, "Featuring the first *great* power ballad of the '90's" in white and "FOREVER" in dark blue. $10

Ludwig Drums, U.S.—Photo of Eric Carr at drum kit; background is beige and shows *Hot in the Shade* LP cover at bottom. $15

S.I.T. Strings, U.S.—Live photo of Bruce Kulick on *Hot in the Shade* stage with the words "Bruce Kulick of KISS" beside him; information about S.I.T. strings at bottom of poster. $12

Revenge CD, U.S.—LP cover with band photo in front of it (from back cover) and black KISS logo at top. $10

Dynasty promotional poster and front of 1990 two-sided poster.

KISS poster showing band with their eyes closed and U.K. promo poster, 1988.

Revenge CD, U.S.—24-inch square poster of LP cover. $10
Revenge CD, U.S.—12-by-36-inch poster; shows part of cover art and says, "Coming May 19" on the right side. $7
Revenge LP, U.K.—Silver logo at top; band photo in center (from back cover of LP); bottom says, "Revenge/Compact Disc—Cassette—Album/Out Now." $20
Revenge LP, U.K.—12-by-36-inch poster has "Revenge" in red, white KISS logo, and "Compact Disc—Cassette—Album/Out Now" in white. $12
"Unholy" single, U.K.—19-by-27.5-inch poster has gray logo at top, "Unholy" in red, and bottom says, "B/W 'God Gave Rock and Roll to You II'/New Single—Out Now" and has a Mercury logo; background is "metal," like LP cover. $15

NON-PROMOTIONAL U.S. POSTERS

Key: Description/Value
Live stage shot, 1975 costumes; Peter Criss is standing up behind the drum kit; "1975 Boutwell" at bottom. $40
Giant 3-by-5-foot poster, collage of live shots from 1975; large stage shot in center; "Boutwell/One Stop Posters/KISS #7" at bottom. $70
Destroyer LP cover art; "Boutwell" at bottom. $20

Destroyer LP cover art on silver foil (heavy paper stock); "Boutwell" at bottom; as advertised on *Rock and Roll Over* merchandise order form. $35

Felt poster of band's faces in circular pattern with logo at bottom; "Pro Arts Inc." at bottom. $20

"U.S. Tour '76" poster; shows band members in *Destroyer* outfits doing parody of "fife and drum" revolutionary war pose; "Exclusive distribution One Stop Posters" at bottom; this poster was later reprinted with the words "U.S. Tour" instead of "U.S. Tour '76," and again later with no wording at the bottom; $20 for 1st edition; $10 for the 2nd edition. $7 for the 3rd edition

Shot of band in *Destroyer* outfits on top of Empire State Building; as advertised on *Love Gun* merchandise order form. $15

Destroyer-era group shot with a member's face in each corner; "Dargis Associates" at bottom. $20

Set of 4 posters: 1 each of Gene, Paul, Ace, and Peter in *Destroyer* outfits, sitting on motorcycles; "Pro Art Inc." at bottom. $15 each; set of 4: $60

Collage poster, shows 4 photos, 1 of each member on motorcycles (same photos as above, but this poster was printed 2 years later); "1979 Aucoin Pro Arts" at bottom. $15

Illustrated poster of monster in Gene's *Destroyer* costume, with Gene's face as the monster's boots; this poster was reprinted years later; "Portal Productions Ltd." at bottom. $7

Love Gun LP cover art on silver foil (heavy paper stock); "Boutwell" at bottom; as advertised on *Love Gun* merchandise order form. $35

Giant 3-by-5-foot poster shows 2 shots (1 live, 1 posed) of each member in *Love Gun* outfits, and has a group shot at top and KISS Army logo at bottom; center photo is a drum kit with the KISS logo over it; "Boutwell/One Stop Posters OSP #407" at bottom. $60

Giant 3-by-5-foot poster has 1977 live shot at top; below that is band in *Love Gun* outfits standing on Plexiglas cubes, with 2 shots (1 live, 1 posed) of each member on the sides of the group shot; "#3001 KISS Love Gun" at bottom. $60

Photos of each member (*Love Gun* outfits), with group shot in center; "20-216 Super KISS" at bottom. $30

Set of 4 posters, each member in *Love Gun* outfits: live shot of Gene, at microphone, with both arms outstretched; posed shot of Paul, crouching down and holding guitar straight out; live shot of Ace with smoking guitar; and a live shot of Peter singing "Beth"; as advertised on *Alive II* merchandise order form. $20 each; set of 4: $80

Love Gun stage shot, taken from far back; as advertised on *Alive II* merchandise order form. $15

Set of 6 Mylar posters (posters were printed in black ink on thin reflective silver plastic known as silver Mylar): 1 group photo in *Destroyer* outfits, 1 group photo in *Love Gun* outfits, and 1 of each member in *Love Gun* outfits; as advertised on the *Double Platinum* merchandise order form. $25 each group poster; $20–25 each individual poster; $150 full set of 6

Group shot of band standing on Plexiglas cubes; logo at top; "Western Graphics Cat. #41" at bottom. $15

Posed *Love Gun* group shot with bluish gray background; Gene is leaning his head back, and Paul has his arm stretched out in front of him; "1790 KISS/Aucoin" at bottom. $25

Set of 4 posters: 1 of each member's solo-LP cover art; as advertised on solo-LP order forms. $25 each; set of 4: $100

All 4 solo LP covers on one poster; as advertised on solo LP merchandise order forms. $20

Black light poster of the illustration used on the back glass of the pinball machine (fuzzy black areas of the poster make it look like a black velvet painting); "C/C Sales, Licensed by NIOCUA Merch." at bottom (NIOCUA is Aucoin spelled backward). $30

Dynasty LP cover art poster, as advertised on *Dynasty* merchandise order form; "C/C Sales—NIOCUA" at bottom. $25

"Superheroes" poster: individual shots of Gene, Paul, Ace, and Peter in *Dynasty* outfits; as advertised on *Unmasked* merchandise order form. $25

Unmasked LP cover art poster, as advertised on *Unmasked* merchandise order form. $30

"Fantasy" Poster (1st poster with Eric Carr): individual shots of Gene, Paul, Ace, and Eric in *Unmasked* outfits; Gene is standing beside a gargoyle, Paul is being touched by lots of female hands, Ace is in a blue neon tunnel, and Eric is swinging on an iron fence. $50

Black light poster of KISS logo (fuzzy black poster with greenish KISS logo); "Funky Enterprise/The KISS Co./KISS Organization" on bottom. $15

Group poster with Mark St. John, white background; says "Funky Ent. KISS Co. #1514" at bottom. $15

Gene 1984 live shot (sold on tour), leaning toward camera and sticking tongue out, red jagged border; "Winterland Rock Express 1985 KISS Company" at bottom. $10

Paul 1984 live shot (sold on tour), leaning on mike stand, orange jagged border; "Winterland Rock Express 1985 KISS Company" at bottom. $10

Group shot with Bruce, blue background with woman's hand "ripping" through poster; "Personalities Inc. 1985 KISS Co." at bottom. $10

Shot of Paul with black leather draped over his shoulder, pink background; "Funky Ent. 1985 KISS Co." at bottom. $10

Collage of *Asylum* photos of each member (GS/PS/EC/BK) with large stage shot in center; "1985 KISS Co. Funky Entertainment #3049" at bottom. $10

Gene live shot at mike, *Asylum* outfit. $8

Paul live shot, playing red guitar, *Asylum* outfit. $8

Collage of *Crazy Nights*–era photos in "glass shards" (not LP cover art); "1988 Winterland" at bottom. $8

1990 Group shot (sold on *Hot in the Shade* tour) with purple background; "Winterland Rock Express" on bottom. $10

NON-PROMOTIONAL FOREIGN POSTERS

Key: Origin/Description/Value

CANADA

1975 live shot, the band just about to do "Deuce" choreography; "WG 2399" at bottom. $30

Illustration of Gene, Paul, Ace, and Peter in *Destroyer* costumes; "#550 Litho by Big Foot" at bottom. $10

Posed *Destroyer* group shot, red background; "Five Star Posters, Vancouver, BC" at bottom. $10

Collage of live shots from 1977 and 1978, with posed group shot in center; "Campus Craft, Edmonton" at bottom. $20

"KISS '79" in big letters at bottom; 1977/1978 photos of each band member; both Paul's and Gene's photos are backward; "1978 Aucoin Management/ Campus Craft, Edmonton, Canada" at bottom. $25

Collage of solo-LP-era photos; "1978 Campus Craft, Edmonton" at bottom. $25

"KISS '80" in big letters at bottom; individual shots of each band member in *Dynasty* outfits (with Peter Criss). $25

Creatures group shot, same as above, but with pink background and yellow border. $10

DENMARK

Live shot of band (late '74/early '75), possibly a photo from the "Midnight Special" TV show. $35

ENGLAND (U.K.)

Shot of Gene, Paul, and Vinnie Vincent on stage tank during *Lick It Up* German tour; "Rebel Rock RE 665" at bottom. $10

Creatures-era group shot with Ace, bluish gray background, "KISS" in Old English script; "Anabas AA212" at bottom. $15

Creatures group shot (with Ace), pink background; Gene, Paul, and Ace are holding guitars, Eric Carr is holding drumsticks; "Anabas AA075" at bottom. $10

1985 photo of band on sidewalk, with large road-construction hole in front of them; "1989 Anabas AA400" at bottom. $15

Live *Love Gun* shot of Gene and Ace back to back; "B218 Big O Publishing" at bottom. $20

Live shot of Gene in 1975 outfit, from Gene's left side; "Big O Productions B199" at bottom. $25

Posed shot of Gene in *Destroyer* costume, standing in front of glittery silver background; "Anabas AA069" at bottom. $15

ITALY

1980 live shot of band (Eric Carr not visible); "1060 Edizioni Quadrifoglio" at
  bottom. $20
Posed shot on stage during *Creatures* era (with Ace); "RB/428 Fotocronache Olympia" at bottom. $25

JAPAN

Polystar *Asylum* poster; 4 photos: 1985 stage shot with logo lit up and sparks flying
  from pinwheels, live shot of Paul pointing at camera, Eric at drum kit giving a
  thumbs-up sign, and a live shot of Gene and Bruce; "Polystar Records and
  Tapes" at bottom (this poster may or may not be promotional). $25

THE NETHERLANDS

Very close-up shot of Gene during *Unmasked* tour; "Rock On PO 022" at bottom.
  $20
1977 shot of band standing on Plexiglas cubes; "Verkerke Reproduckties #1174"
  at bottom. $20

SCOTLAND

Poster shows two *Creatures*-era shots: 1 of band with red background, and 1 of
  Gene with red background; "Holmes McDougall #3437" at bottom. $20
1976 shot of band on motorcycles; "Holmes McDougall #86/P3171" at bottom.
  $25
1977 shot of Gene at microphone, about to stick out tongue; "Holmes McDougall
  Ltd. #314/P3268" at bottom. $25
35-by-49-inch collage poster; 1977 group shot at top, center photo is Gene standing
  behind a spiderweb; "Holmes McDougall 3/P7019" at bottom. $35
Posed *Love Gun* stage shot; "Holmes McDougall 95/P3236" at bottom. $30
35-by-49-inch 1975 stage shot, Gene at mike on left, Ace and Paul at mike on right;
  "Holmes McDougall G5/P7005" at bottom. $30

SWITZERLAND

1975 shot of Gene from the knees up, spitting blood; "Wizard & Genius 2637"
  at bottom. $25
1976 shot of Paul on motorcycle (different from U.S. poster pose); "Wizard &
  Genius WG2400" at bottom. $25
1978 shot (from *Phantom* movie) of Gene picking up the dragon stage prop; "Wizard & Genius WG 2490" at bottom. $30

UNKNOWN COUNTRY

Posed group poster with Vinnie Vincent, no makeup, red background. $15

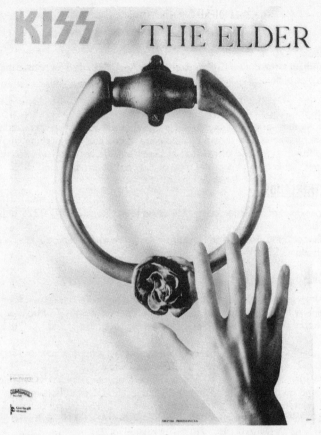

Clear plastic promotional poster for (*Music from*) *The Elder* (U.S.).

PHOTOS

It is impossible to list the value of every KISS photo ever taken, but we have put together a rule of thumb for KISS photos, based on year taken, size, and whether the photo was promotional. Promotional photos are easily recognizable because they have the band's name, and sometimes other information, printed in the border of the photo. Promotional photographs are made for use alone or in press kits, which are then used by newspapers and magazines when they need photos and background information about the band. Press kits are sometimes also sent to radio stations. Press kits themselves are collectible, and you can find them listed in ''Promotional Merchandise.''

PROMOTIONAL PHOTOS

Years	8x10 Black & White	Value	8x10 Color
1973–1978	$6–8		$8–10
1979–1983	$5–7		$6–8
1984–1993	$4–6		$5–7

Sizes refer to size in inches (8x10 = eight inches by ten inches). These values are only a guideline, and the actual value of a photograph also depends on its rareness, quality, and condition (see page 110).

NON-PROMOTIONAL PHOTOS

Regular (non-promo) photos are any photos of KISS, taken by anyone, that are not officially released by KISS for promotional use. (By photo, we are referring to actual photographs, not pictures torn out of magazines.) We have broken down this category by size (in inches), as regular photos are almost always color. Again, value also depends on the rareness, quality, and condition of the photograph (see page 110).

Years	8x10	Value 5x7	3.5x5
1973–1978	$4–5	$3–4	$2–3
1979–1983	$3–4	$2–3	$1–2
1984–1993	$2–3	$1–2	$.50–1.50

There are 3 criteria you should use to determine the value of a photograph:

Rareness: Is it a picture of Gene's hair on fire? Is Paul wearing the "bandit" makeup (his earliest makeup)? Is it a shot of Eric Carr from his 1st show at the Palladium when his makeup was different (no white stripe down his nose)? Anything like that can make a photo more rare than, for example, a shot of Ace onstage, playing guitar.

Quality: How close-up was the photo taken? How clear is it? Do the colors look right? These are some of the ways to determine the quality of a photograph. If you can see the KISS logos on the guitar picks, it's probably a good-quality photograph.

Condition: Does the photo look like it has been bent or ripped anywhere? Has it been written on or otherwise damaged? That lowers the value of the photograph.

The prices listed on page 109 are only a guide. If a photo is particularly rare or particularly well shot, it may demand a higher price. Also, if the photo was taken by a well-known photographer, its price may be somewhat higher. The other factor that we cannot figure in but which always affects price is the *how-bad-do-you-want-it?* factor. If, for whatever reason, you think that a photo is worth $10 or $15, then it is worth that . . . to you. That's why these prices are never a hard and fast rule.

POSTCARDS AND STICKERS

There are probably many KISS postcards that were manufactured without KISS's express permission, especially in countries other than the United States. Postcards are generally not broken down into categories of "official" and "bootleg," because it's difficult to tell and there is not a significant difference in the quality or value. There are only a few official stickers, but they tend to be of much better quality than bootleg stickers. The following is a partial list of KISS postcards and stickers, with approximate values (assuming mint condition).

Postcard—*KISS* LP cover art (first album). $3

Postcard—Posed 1975 shot with red background (Gene and Peter on top; Ace and Paul on the bottom). $3

Postcard—White with reproduction of pink concert poster advertising a June 1976 Zurich, Switzerland, show; poster has caricatures of band's faces. $3

Postcard—1976 live shot of band (*Destroyer* outfits) coming out to take their bows. $3

Postcard—1976 live shot of Gene (*Destroyer* outfit) at microphone; shot taken from the floor. $3

Postcard—*Destroyer* LP cover art. $3

Postcard—Same as *Love Gun*–era collage poster (with KISS Army logo). $3

Postcard—*Dynasty* LP cover art. $3

Postcard—Paul (*Dynasty* outfit) in front of microphone, right arm raised. $3

Postcard—1982 band shot (G/P/AF/EC) with pink background. $3

Postcard—Gene, live shot (*Creatures of the Night* outfit) with bloody bass axe. $3

Postcard—Vinnie Vincent (*Creatures of the Night* outfit) with Flying V. $3

Postcard—Reddish postcard says, "Unmasked Tour" vertically across the middle, and shows 4 photos: Vinnie during *Lick It Up* tour, blurry shot of stage with lighted logo, 1980 shot of Gene breathing fire, and Paul during *Lick It Up* tour with zebra-striped Flying V guitar. $3

Postcard—"Asylum" and German KISS logo and 4 small photos: Gene during *Lick It Up* video, Paul during *Heaven's On Fire* video, a live *Animalize* shot of Eric, and a live *Animalize* shot of Bruce. $3

Postcard—Yellow German KISS logo at top, "Animalize" in red, and "Tour '84" in white at bottom. Photos are live shots of Paul and the whole band from 1983, and the back-cover photo from the *Animalize* LP. $3

Postcard—*Crazy Nights* LP cover art. $3

Postcard—Same as *Crazy Nights*–era poster: glass shards with pictures of band members in the pieces of glass. $3

Postcard—Promo postcard for *Hot in the Shade*; front shows LP cover, back encourages recipients to call radio stations and M-TV. $8

Sticker postcard (Post A Stickercard)—Paul, same as his official *Animalize* poster (sticker is from Switzerland). $4

Sticker postcard (Post A Stickercard)—Gene, same as his official *Animalize* poster (sticker is from Switzerland). $4

Giant postcard (12 by 16 inches)—Live shot of Gene, Paul, and Vinnie from the *Creatures* tour. $6

Giant postcard (12 by 16 inches)—Live shot of Paul from *Lick It Up* tour (on the back of the postcard, Paul is identified as "Gene Simmons"). $6

Note card—This was a square cardboard envelope with the *Destroyer* cover art on it, and it held a record-shaped piece of "notepaper" on which to write a letter. $12

Sticker—*Destroyer* cover art; this sticker looks exactly like the LP cover and should not be confused with bootleg stickers with similar artwork; Sticker is 5 inches square. $10

Sticker—*Rock and Roll Over* sticker from LP. $5

Stickers—Puffy stickers (Rockstics); set of 4, 1 each of Gene, Paul, Ace, and Peter. $10 each, $45/set (sealed)

Stickers—Poster Put-Ons; set of 3, 1 each of *Love Gun* cover art, *Alive II* stage shot (says "Live II"), and the "U.S. Tour '76" photo. $8–10 each, $30/set (sealed)

Bumper sticker—*Animalize*. $3–5

Bootleg stickers—In general, these are worth about $1–2, and the price is based on the quality of the sticker and the artwork.

KISS postcards and stickers

OFFICIAL T-SHIRTS AND IRON-ON TRANSFERS

The following list of official T-shirts is by no means complete. In their 20-year history, KISS has released many dozens of official T-shirts, which were sold in many different parts of the world. The earliest shirts were done as iron-ons, but after T-shirt silkscreening techniques were developed, iron-on transfers began to be phased out (around 1978/1979). In the early 1980s, photo-silkscreening started to be used, further increasing the quality of rock T-shirts.

Unused iron-ons (not fused onto T-shirts) are not as collectible as the T-shirt with iron-ons on them, as they're harder to store properly and it's harder to view the image. Nonetheless, if you have unused iron-ons, it's not usually a good idea to try to iron them onto T-shirts unless you have a machine made for that purpose, as iron-ons are often ruined when you attempt to iron them onto shirts. Most mint-quality unused KISS iron-ons are worth around $6–7.

To determine whether a KISS T-shirt is official, look for fine print at the side or bottom of the image that says © 1977 Aucoin Management; or © 1979 in Association With KISS, a Partnership; or © 1986 the KISS Company; or © 1990 Winterland Productions; or anything along those lines. If there is no such copyright information on the T-shirt, it is probably not official, although some early iron-ons did not have copyright information on them. In the following list, most of the iron-ons don't have a shirt color listed, as the shirt color was usually chosen by the purchaser of the transfer.

Here is a partial list of KISS official T-shirts and their values; remember that value is based on age, quantity printed, and quality of the shirt and its design. For iron-ons, the values are for the iron-on *on* a shirt, not the transfer alone. All values assume **MINT** condition.

IRON-ONS

1974 live shot with orange logo at top, "in concert" at bottom, and orange "splash" border. $20

Collage of photos from the *Alive!* booklet, with logo at top. $20

Cover art of *Alive!*, irregular-shape border; says "76 Aucoin/Boutwell" at bottom. $18

KISS Army logo (glitter iron-on). $14

Original members in front of the Hollywood Wax Museum. $18

Destroyer cover art. $16

Set of 4 transfers: 1 of each original member in *Destroyer* outfits, sitting on motorcycles. $18 each

1975 costumes shot, in which band members all have their eyes closed; photo seems to be breaking through a piece of metal; copyright says, "Allstar Heat Transfer Corp. 1977." $18

Black T-shirt with multicolored logo (from *Rock and Roll Over* order form). $17

Logo with each member in 1 letter (AF/PS/GS/PC); (from *Dynasty* order form). $16

Logo with each member in 1 letter (AF/PS/GS/EC). $18

Tan T-shirt with *Love Gun* cover art (from *Love Gun* order form). $18

Love Gun photo (left to right, PS/GS/AF/PC) with blue, green, and red border with logo at bottom; copyright says, "Aucoin 1977 in partnership with KISS." $18

1977 stage shot (same as live shot on garbage can), with "marquee lights" around the photo. $18

Love Gun–era photo with band on Plexiglas cubes; yellow/red border; red logo with yellow outline at bottom. $18

Circular photo of Paul with illustration of Paul at bottom; glitter iron-on; copyright says, "1979 Aucoin by Agreement with KISS/P. Stanley, Photo-Lith." $18

Circular photo of Gene with illustration of Gene at bottom; glitter iron-on; copyright says, "1979 Aucoin by Agreement with KISS/G. Simmons, Photo-Lith." $18

Circular photo of Ace with illustration of Ace at bottom; glitter iron-on; copyright says, "1979 Aucoin by Agreement with KISS/A. Frehley, Photo-Lith." $18

Circular photo of Peter with illustration of Peter at bottom; glitter iron-on; copyright says, "1979 Aucoin by Agreement with KISS/P. Criss, Photo-Lith." $18

Cover of all 4 solo album covers; copyright says, "1978 Aucoin Management with KISS, A Partnership." $15

Photo of Gene in *Dynasty* outfit with bass axe; logo is red; glitter iron-on on red shirt. $18

Photo of Paul in *Dynasty* outfit; logo is purple; glitter iron-on on purple shirt. $18

Photo of Ace in *Dynasty* outfit; logo is blue; glitter iron-on on blue shirt. $18

Photo of Peter in *Dynasty* outfit; logo is green; glitter iron-on on green shirt. $18

Circular photo of Eric Carr with illustration of Eric at bottom; glitter iron-on; copyright says, "1980 Aucoin by Agreement with KISS/E. Carr." $20

SILKSCREENED T-SHIRTS

Yellow T-shirt with *Rock and Roll Over* cover art. $20

Black T-shirt for the L.A. Forum concerts where *Alive II* was recorded; silver print says, "I Was There" (using slashed *s* in the word "Was"). $45

Black T-shirt with white print that says, "Alive II Tour." $30

Beige T-shirt with "Alive II U.S. tour '77–'78" and small photo of each member (*Unmasked* order form). $35

Black T-shirt with silkscreen of Paul's solo LP cover. $20

Black T-shirt with silkscreen of Gene's solo LP cover. $20

Black T-shirt with silkscreen of Ace Frehley's solo LP cover. $20

Black T-shirt with silkscreen of Peter Criss's solo LP cover. $20

Black T-shirt with silkscreen of all 4 solo LP covers. $20

Black T-shirt with silver KISS logo (from *Double Platinum* order form). $20

Black T-shirt with *Double Platinum* logo in silver and red (from *Double Platinum* order form). $20

Black T-shirt with *Dynasty* LP cover; square border of red and white KISS logos (1st advertised on *Dynasty* order form, 1st pictured on *Unmasked* order form). $25

Black T-shirt with *Dynasty* LP cover; round border of red and white KISS logos; "World Tour 79" in green and blue. $25

Beige T-shirt with *Dynasty* LP cover; square border of red and black KISS logos; black print says, "Return of KISS" and "World Tour 1979." $27

White T-shirt with yellow three-quarter sleeves; front shows *Dynasty* cover art with round border of KISS logos; back has KISS logo at top and illustration of band below (from *Unmasked* order form). $30

Black T-shirt with "Gasp" panel from *Unmasked* cover art (*Unmasked* order form). $20

Black T-shirt for KISS's 1980 Palladium show (New York/Eric Carr's 1st show); red KISS logo with silver trim and silver letters that say, "The Palladium/New York City/July 25, 1980"; back says, "A Night to Remember" in silver. $45

Beige T-shirt with photo-silkscreen of posed stage shot from Palladium. $22

White T-shirt with blue three-quarter sleeves; photo-silkscreen of posed stage shot from Palladium (same as above). $24

Black T-shirt with logo and group photo from *Dynasty* poster, except that Eric's face has been airbrushed over Peter's (KISS Army order form). $30

White T-shirt with black three-quarter sleeves; illustration of Paul, Gene, Ace, and Eric Carr on front, and logo on back (KISS Army order form). $30

Black sweatshirt with small silver KISS logo (KISS Army order form). $45

White T-shirt with black three-quarter sleeves; photo-silkscreen of band (G/P/EC/VV); picture of tank on back; "10th Anniversary Tour" written on both front and back. $30

Black T-shirt for U.K. *Lick It Up* tour; front shows tank and says "World Tour '83–'84"; back shows KISS Army logo and lists the European countries of the tour. $40

Gray T-shirt with blue three-quarter sleeves; *Lick It Up* LP cover art with logo above and "World Tour '83–'84" on bottom; back shows tank and says, "World Tour 1983–1984." $20

Black T-shirt with *Lick It Up* LP cover art and "World Tour '83–'84" on bottom; back says, "If It's Too Loud, You're Too Old." $20

Black T-shirt with "Slave Girl" on front; bass axe and Flying V guitars crossed on back; says, "World Tour '84" on bottom. $20

Gray T-shirt with band photo (G/P/EC/Mark St. John—back cover photo from *Animalize*) and zebra-striped logo and "Animalize" written in red; back says, "Tour '84–'85." $20

Gray T-shirt, same as above, but with Bruce Kulick's face airbrushed over Mark St. John's. $20

White T-shirt with red short sleeves; zebra-striped logo being "ripped" by woman's fingers; "Animalize" in red at bottom; back shows same zebra-striped logo and "Animalize Tour '84–'85" in red. $20

Black T-shirt with *Asylum* LP cover art on front; back says, "Asylum World Tour '85–'86" in blue and red. $17

White T-shirt with black three-quarter sleeves; illustration of band standing underneath blue logo with black outline; back says, "Asylum World Tour '85–'86" in blue and red. $18

White T-shirt with "exploding" KISS logo on front; back says, "Asylum World Tour '85–'86" in blue and red. $17

White T-shirt with *Crazy Nights* LP cover art and logo above it; back says, "I Went Crazy With KISS" in black. $15

White T-shirt with KISS logo on front and 1 member in each letter of the logo (P/BK/G/EC), and woman at bottom; back shows Chikara symbol in black. $15

White T-shirt with KISS logo on front and illustrations of parts of women's bodies in each letter of the logo; back shows Chikara symbol in black. $15

Black T-shirt with illustration of Gene, seated, with women around the chair and a red logo; back says, "It's a Dirty Job, But Somebody's Got to Do It," and includes Gene's autograph in red and white. $14

Black T-shirt with photo-silkscreen of Gene with "face" bass and yellow logo; back says, "It's a Dirty Job, But Somebody's Got to Do It," and includes Gene's autograph in red and white. $16

Black T-shirt with illustration of Paul and 2 women and pink logo; back says, "Life Is Like Sex—The More You Put Into It, The More You Get Out of It," and includes Paul's autograph in pink and white. $14

Black T-shirt with photo-silkscreen of Paul with guitar and yellow logo; back says, "Life Is Like Sex—The More You Put Into It, The More You Get Out of It," and includes Paul's autograph in pink and white. $16

Black T-shirt with band and Chikara symbol on front, with red logo above band; bottom says, "Crazy Nights '88"; back says, "I Went Crazy With KISS" in white. $15

Black T-shirt with *Crazy Nights* LP cover; back has white Chikara symbol. $15

Black T-shirt for Monsters of Rock 1988 concert with Iron Maiden, KISS, David Lee Roth, Megadeth, Guns 'N' Roses, and Helloween; back says, "Monsters of Rock/20th August 1988/Donington Park." $22

Black T-shirt with photo-silkscreen of Paul and the words "Paul Stanley" in yellow around his head; back says, "Rock Express" in green and "Guitar Greats" in yellow, with red outlines of guitars behind the lettering. $20

White sweatshirt with small KISS logo and the word "Forever" in red on the front and the *Hot in the Shade* cover art on the back; this was a *promotional* sweatshirt for *Hot in the Shade*, and it was not for sale to the general public. $75

Black T-shirt with metallic silver logo and photo-silkscreen of band; back shows *Hot in the Shade* "postmark" in silver. $20

Gray T-shirt with Sphinx on front and "Hot in the Shade" below; back has "postmark" in orange. $18

White T-shirt with photo-silkscreen of band (with illustration to make them appear to be standing in knee-deep water) with Sphinx behind them and logo at top; back has "postmark" in pink and tour dates (several versions of this shirt are available; the only difference is the tour dates on the back). $20

Gray T-shirt with fanged Sphinx and "Hot in the Shade" at bottom in yellow, and yellow/orange logo at top; back has "postmark" in red and tour dates. $18

White T-shirt with Egyptian headpiece (like a King Tut burial mask) with sunglasses and fangs, "Hot in the Shade Tour 1990" at bottom and yellow and red logo at top; back says, "Hot N Hard" in red. $18

Black T-shirt with Egyptian headpiece (like a King Tut burial mask) with sunglasses and fangs, "Hot in the Shade Tour 1990" at bottom and yellow and red logo at top; back says, "Hot N Hard" in red. $18

White *tank top* with Egyptian headpiece (like a King Tut burial mask) with sunglasses and fangs, "Hot in the Shade Tour 1990" at bottom and yellow and red logo at top; back says, "Hot N Hard" in red. $20

Black *tank top* with Egyptian headpiece (like a King Tut burial mask) with sunglasses and fangs, "Hot in the Shade Tour 1990" at bottom and yellow and red logo at top; back says, "Hot N Hard" in red. $20

1991 Winterland reissue black T-shirt with *Destroyer* cover art on front; "Destroyer" written in orangish letters on back. $15

1992 Winterland reissue black T-shirt with solo LPs cover art on front; neon green logo on back. $15

Black T-shirt with photo-silkscreen of band (PS/GS/BK/ES) with silver logo filled with red skulls; back says, "Revenge" in red. $22

White T-shirt with same picture as above, but illustrated; silver logo filled with red skulls; back says, "Revenge World Tour 1992" in black. $22

Black T-shirt with photo-silkscreen of skull with horns; logo written diagonally beside skull and the word "Unholy" surrounds it; back has KISS logo and the lyrics to "Unholy." $20

White T-shirt with teal and black "all-over" silkscreen; band and color splotches are all over the shirt; from the *Revenge* tour. $30

PAUL STANLEY 1989 SOLO TOUR T-SHIRTS

Black T-shirt with Paul in black robe with spiderweb behind him, "Paul Stanley" in red and yellow letters above him; back says, "I Had a One-Night Stand" in red and yellow letters. $25

Black T-shirt with photo-silkscreen of Paul and "Paul Stanley" written vertically in yellow and blue letters on the left; the back says, "I Had a One-Night Stand" in yellow and blue letters. $25

Black T-shirt with two crossed guitars, feathers on the sides, a dagger in the center, and a green banner below that says, "Who Dares Wins" in black; "Paul Stanley" written at top in blue and red letters; back says, "I Had a One-Night Stand" in blue and red letters. $25

BOOTLEG T-SHIRTS

It is usually pretty easy to identify bootleg T-shirts. They don't contain official licensing wording such as "Aucoin Management 1977" or "Rock Steady," and there is usually no registered trademark symbol by the KISS logo. They are usually of inferior quality compared to official merchandise. Also, if the pictures on the front and back are not from the same era, it is a bootleg (i.e., if the front is the cover of the *Asylum* album, and the back is a *Destroyer* photo). They are not as valuable as official T-shirts, so bootleg T-shirts are generally only worth $3–10, depending on the quality of the artwork.

OFFICIAL HATS

Item/Year	Value
Black hat with silver KISS logo patch, 1977	$15
'83/'84 black tour hat with tank, 1983	$20
Hot in the Shade promotional black corduroy hat, 1990	$20
Black hat with fluorescent green logo, 1992	$10
Black hat with silver-gray silkscreened logo, 1992	$17

Hats: (l. to r.) 1977 hat with silver logo, 1983 tour hat with tank, and promotional *Hot in the Shade* corduroy hat with embroidered Sphinx

BOOTLEG HATS

Bootleg hats are generally worth about $3–7, depending on the quality of the artwork. Official patches sewn onto hats (a common practice) are considered bootleg hats and are worth about $2–3 more than the patch alone.

OFFICIAL SCARVES, BANDANNAS, AND HEADBANDS

Satin scarf—White with white fringe at ends; red print says, "KISS European Tour" and shows photos of Gene, Paul, Eric Carr, and Vinnie Vincent. Two types exist: shiny satin finish and dull nylon finish. $10

Satin scarf—Black with black fringe at ends; gold print says, "KISS European Tour" and shows photos of Gene, Paul, Eric Carr, and Vinnie Vincent. $10

Satin scarf—Black with red fringe at ends; gold print says, "1983/KISS World Tour/1984." $15

Knit scarf—Black with red edges; gold print says, "1984/KISS World Tour/1985." $35

Cotton scarf—White with black zebra stripes; has leopard-print logos at ends, and "Animalize" written in yellow. $8

Bandanna—Black with red KISS logos. $10

Bandanna—Red with black KISS logos. $10

Bandanna—White with black zebra stripes, leopard-print logos, and "Animalize" written in yellow. $7

Bandanna—Asylum cover art. $10
*Bandanna—*Sphinx and *Hot in the Shade* "postmark." $10
Bandanna—"Revenge" written diagonally in red across "metal"-look background; large KISS logos in each corner. $10
*Headband—*Brown with black zebra stripe and yellow logo. $4

BOOTLEG SCARVES, BANDANNAS, AND HEADBANDS

The value of bootleg items depends almost completely on the quality of the item. Bootleg KISS scarves, bandannas, and headbands are generally worth about $1–5, depending on their quality.

KISS scarves, bandannas, and headbands—official and bootleg.

JEWELRY, PINS, AND PATCHES

OFFICIAL JEWELRY

The following is a list of official KISS jewelry with original prices and current values. For items that were available through the mail, the ''Where Advertised'' column lists either the KISS album merchandise order form (MOF) that offered the item for sale, or the magazine(s) that contained offers for the merchandise.

Item	Year	Where Advertised	Original Price	Value
Gold logo necklace	1977	Love Gun/Alive II	$8.50	$10
Silver logo necklace	1978	Double Platinum MOF	$6	$12
Logo necklace, gold with red enamel	1978	Solo LP MOFs & Dynasty MOF	$5	$6
Signature necklace, (PS/GS/AF/PC)	1978	Solo LP MOFs	$5	$20
Signature stickpins	1978	Various magazines	$?	$15
Logo stickpins, gold or silver	1980	Unmasked MOF	$5.50	$12
Logo bracelet, gold	1978	KISS Meets the Phantom Magazine	$5	$12
Costume jewelry: ring (GS/PS/AF/PC/group)	1978–79	Various magazines	$2	$15
Costume jewelry: bracelet (GS/PS/AF/PC/group)	1978–79	Various magazines	$3	$15
Costume jewelry: necklace (GS/PS/AF/PC/group)	1978–79	Various magazines	$3	$15
Silver necklace with dragon boot and logo	1980	Sold in stores	$5	$20
Silver necklace with maltese cross and logo	1980	Sold in stores	$5	$20

Item	Year	Where Advertised	Original Price	Value
Silver necklace with lightning bolt and logo	1980	Sold in stores	$5	$20

Authors' note: Bracelets and necklaces described as "costume jewelry" consisted of two-sided KISS "charms" attached to necklaces or bracelets. The "costume jewelry" rings were cheap metal rings with KISS pictures glued to them.

BOOTLEG JEWELRY

Because bootleg jewelry can be made at any time in any quantity, it is seldom worth very much. There are bootleg KISS logo necklaces, necklaces with Gene's face (usually with a tongue hanging out), KISS logo earrings, and various other pieces of unofficial KISS jewelry. Most pieces are worth only $1–3, unless it's a particularly well-made or unusual item. In general, pay what you think it's worth.

Official KISS jewelry and belt buckles

Some official KISS pins

OFFICIAL BELT BUCKLES

The following is the complete list of official KISS belt buckles, along with their value and the order form that offered the item for sale. Values are for mint-quality belt buckles.

Description	Value	Album (Order Form)
Black with silver logo	$12	*Rock and Roll Over, Love Gun, Alive II, Double Platinum*
Destroyer (cover art)	$20	*Destroyer* tourbook order form
Rock and Roll Over (cover art)	$20	*Rock and Roll Over*
Love Gun (cover art)	$20	*Love Gun*
Paul Stanley (illustration from *Love Gun* cover, with autograph)	$20	Solo LPs
Gene Simmons (illustration from *Love Gun* cover, with autograph)	$20	Solo LPs

Description	Value	Album (Order Form)
Ace Frehley (illustration from *Love Gun* cover, with autograph)	$20	Solo LPs
Peter Criss (illustration from *Love Gun* cover, with autograph)	$20	Solo LPs
Large Brass KISS logo	$15	*Alive II*
Large KISS logo with chrome finish	$15	*Double Platinum*
Oval buckle with blue logo and light green background	$12	
Oval buckle with reflective red background, gold triangle, and reflective gold logo	$12	
Oval "Fantasia" buckle—dark blue background, red/orange logo, and winged demon	$15	

BOOTLEG BELT BUCKLES

There are a lot of bootleg KISS belt buckles, and they are generally worth about $3–10, depending on the quality of the artwork and the quality of the buckle itself.

PINS (BUTTONS/BADGES)

Pins are generally not expensive items, and little distinction is usually made between bootleg and official pins. Official pins will have some kind of copyright information (i.e., "copyright 1985 The KISS Organization") printed in fine print on the side or bottom of the pin. We have drawn up some guidelines as to the worth of KISS pins, but these are only guidelines. . . . If you see a pin that is very unusual or particularly attractive, you would pay more for it than a very ordinary or unattractive pin. The guidelines on page 125 assume that "small pins" are 2 inches in diameter or less, and that pins larger than that are "large."

	Small	**Large**
Pins with makeup:	$1–2	$3–4
Pins without makeup:	$.50–1	$1.50–2

If a pin is official, add $1–2 to the above price.

Some interesting KISS pins:

The "I Was There" pin—This pin, like the "I Was There" T-shirt, was sold at the concerts where *Alive II* was recorded. $10–12

Official logo pin—A 3-inch black pin with a red/orange KISS logo, this official pin was released in late 1979 or early 1980. $6

OFFICIAL PATCHES AND BACKPATCHES

Small black patch with silver KISS logo (as seen on *Love Gun* merchandise order form and several subsequent order forms). $5

Small KISS Army patch (red/yellow/black); this patch was offered for sale on the *Unmasked* order form. $4

"If It's Too Loud, You're Too Old" Backpatch; black backpatch with white logo and red lettering, by Winterland Express, 1989; came sealed on cardboard. $7–9

Small black patch, silver logo with blue outline; this patch was released by Winterland in 1992. $3

BOOTLEG PATCHES AND BACKPATCHES

All other patches are bootlegs, and the small ones (less than 6 inches in any direction) are worth about $2–4 each, depending on the quality. Medium patches (smaller than backpatches, but bigger than 6 inches in one or more directions) are worth about $4–5. Bootleg backpatches, depending on their quality, are worth $3–10.

KISS patches and backpatches

PROMOTIONAL MERCHANDISE

U.S. PROMOTIONAL MERCHANDISE

(For promotional posters, see "Posters, Photos, and Postcards")

Album flats: with makeup—$10–12; without makeup—$3–5
Press kits: with makeup—$40–50; without makeup—$10–15. From at least *Destroyer* until *Creatures of the Night*, the press kits came with a full-color folder that looked like the LP cover. Inside were between 1 and 5 photos, a biography, and sometimes other related material. (The solo LPs had one press kit that covered the 4 LPs.) After *Creatures*, the folders were not used, and press kits generally consisted of a quickie bio, 1–5 photos, and sometimes a discography.

PROMOTIONAL ITEMS FOR PARTICULAR ALBUMS

Hotter than Hell: 2-sided 3-D cardboard hanging mobile; photo of band from LP cover with "explosions" in front of band. $90–100
Destroyer: 5-inch square promotional sticker (LP cover art). $10
Alive!: Cardboard hanging mobile. $120
Love Gun: Cardboard stand-up of band from LP cover; 3 feet tall. $100–110
Alive II: Cardboard hanging mobile with small LP covers hanging off it. $125
Double Platinum: Black cardboard arrow (approximately 2.5 feet long) with silver KISS logo and the words "Double Platinum" in red. $30–35
   Silver cardboard logo (approx. 2.5 feet long) with "Double Platinum" written in red. $35–40
   2-sided silver cardboard logo (folds flat). $45–50
   (These items match the silver/black/red *Double Platinum* promotional poster; see "The Merchandise.")
Solo LPs: 4-foot-square cardboard wall hanging (folds in half); cover art of all 4 solo LPs. $150
   2-foot-square cardboard wall hanging; cover art of all 4 solo LPs. $25
   20-inch cardboard arrow with cover art of all 4 solo LPs. $25
Dynasty: 4-foot-square cardboard wall hanging (folds in half); *Dynasty* cover art. $150
   4-foot silver cardboard strip with 3 KISS logos on each side (2 black and 1 red). $35

Unmasked: 12-inch cardboard cube; LP cover art on 2 sides, pictures of KISS LPs
    on 2 sides, and KISS logo on top and bottom. $70
Smashes, Thrashes and Hits: Triangular cardboard stand-up; medium size—$20;
    large size—$25.
    3-D cardboard poster-size stand-up. $50
Hot in the Shade: Promotional black corduroy baseball cap with Sphinx design.
    $25
    Promotional white "Forever" sweatshirt. $75
    Triangular Cardboard Sphinx stand-up (small). $20

IN-HOUSE PROMOTIONAL ITEMS

These items were not distributed to record stores or radio
stations as a promotion, but were given to KISS Company and/
or Polygram Records employees to commemorate the release of
different KISS albums. They are very rare collector's items.

Hot in the Shade promotional pyramid-shaped paperweight (was only given to
    Polygram employees); very rare. $100
Promotional jackets—For at least the last few KISS LP releases, jackets with the
    album logo have been issued to employees of KISS Company and other KISS
    personnel. For example, the *Hot in the Shade* jacket was a black leather jacket
    with the Sphinx embroidered on the back. These jackets are very rare and are
    worth about $350–400 each.

FOREIGN PROMOTIONAL MERCHANDISE

There has probably been as much promotional material for
KISS outside the U.S. as there has been in the U.S., but trying
to catalog all of it is an impossible task. This is a partial list of
items used to promote KISS in other countries:

Press kits: Europe (with makeup)—$55   Europe (without)—$20
            Australia (with)—$55   Australia (without)—$20
            Japan (with)—$60   Japan (without)—$25

Attack of the Phantoms movie (theatrical release):

> *Lobby cards*—These 8-by-10-inch or oversize color photos were used to line the lobby of the theater that showed the film. They are worth about $10–20, depending on the size, how good the photo is, and whether the members of KISS appear in the photo.

> *Promotional posters*—These posters, which range from very small to poster size (2 by 3 feet) to extra large (3 by 4 feet), were used by the theater to promote the film. Different countries would have different posters; for example, the British *Attack of the Phantoms* poster has an orange background and a 1978 band shot, while the German poster has a blue background and shows photos from the *Dynasty* LP cover. In general, the small posters are worth $12–20, and average or large posters, $35–50.

Crazy Nights *LP*—3-D cardboard wall hanging, 18 inches square. Shows cover art of LP, with extra pieces at the corners to make it "3-D." $35

Crazy Nights *U.K. tour promotional mug*—This white coffee mug has black print that shows photos of Paul, Gene, Eric Carr, and Bruce Kulick, along with the words "MCP presents Crazy Nights 1988," a huge white KISS logo, and "plus special guests Kings of the Sun." $25

Cardboard promotional items

Backstage passes

BACKSTAGE PASSES

Opposite are some of the backstage passes used on past KISS tours. The 1st list refers to satin passes, which are fabric passes with adhesive backing. The 2nd list refers to laminated passes, or "laminates." Laminated passes were generally given to road crew and security personnel who would use them for the entire tour. Authentic KISS passes made after 1982 were made by the Otto company, and will have the Otto logo on the back (and in many cases, on the front in small letters). These lists are *not* complete.

SATIN BACKSTAGE PASSES

Year/Tour	Shape/Color	Wording/Status	Value
'74/Hotter Than Hell	Square/Red	Special guest	$15
'75/Dressed to Kill	Rectangle/Blue	Spring Tour '75	$15
'75/Dressed to Kill	Square/B & W	(LP cover art)	$15
'77/Love Gun	Square/Blue	KISS All World Tour 1977–1978	$14
'77–'78/Love Gun	Circle/Green	KISS All World Tour 1977–1978	$14
'79/Dynasty	Square/Gray	The Return of KISS (LP poster art)	$14
'79/Dynasty	Square/B & W	The Return of KISS (LP cover art)	$12
'80/Unmasked	Rectangle/Red	KISS World Tour 1980/VIP	$13
'80/Unmasked	Rectangle/Red	KISS World Tour 1980/ House Only	$11
'83/Creatures of the Night	Square/Red	10th KISS Anniversary Tour/ VIP	$11
'83/Creatures of the Night	Square/Black	10th KISS Anniversary Tour	$11
'83/Creatures of the Night	Square/Orange	10th KISS Anniversary Tour/ Photo/Press	$11
'83–'84/Lick It Up	Rectangle/Green	KISS United States Tour 1983/84/Crew	$10
'83–'84/Lick It Up	Rectangle/Blue	KISS United States Tour 1983/84/Guest	$10
'83–'84/Lick It Up	Rectangle/ Orange	KISS United States Tour 1983/84/Guest	$10
'83–'84/Lick It Up	Rectangle/Red	KISS United States Tour 1983/84/Press	$10
'83–'84/Lick It Up	Rectangle/Purple	KISS United States Tour 1983/84	$10
'84/Animalize	Rectangle/B & W	KISS 1984 Tour of Europe & the U.K./Press	$11
'84/Animalize	Rectangle/Yellow	Animalize World Tour 84–85/VIP	$10
'84/Animalize	Rectangle/Blue	Animalize World Tour 84–85/Crew	$10
'85/Asylum	Rectangle/No border	KISS Asylum (illus. of band)/ Photo	$8
'85/Asylum	Rectangle/Green border	KISS Asylum (illus. of band)/ Guest	$8

Year/Tour	Shape/Color	Wording/Status	Value
'87–'88/Crazy Nights	Rectangle/ Orange	KISS Crazy Nights/Guest	$8
'87–'88/Crazy Nights	Rectangle/Green	KISS Crazy Nights/Photo	$8
'87–'88/Crazy Nights	Rectangle/Black	KISS Crazy Nights/Crew	$8
'87–'88/Crazy Nights	Triangle/Pink	KISS Crazy Nights/Guest	$8
'87–'88/Crazy Nights	Triangle/Black	KISS Crazy Nights/Guest	$8
'88/Crazy Nights	Circle/Red	KISS Crazy Nights Europe 88/After Show	$10
'88/Crazy Nights	Triangle/Orange	KISS Crazy Nights Europe 88/All Access	$10
'88/Crazy Nights	Triangle/Blue	KISS Crazy Nights Europe 88/All Access	$10
'90/Hot in the Shade	Round/Black	KISS Hot in the Shade/Photo	$7
'90/Hot in the Shade	Rectangle/Red	KISS Hot in the Shade/Pre-show	$7
'90/Hot in the Shade	Rectangle/Green	KISS Hot in the Shade/Pre-Show	$7
'90/Hot in the Shade	Diamond/Red	KISS Hot in the Shade/After Show	$7
'90/Hot in the Shade	Octagon/Orange	KISS Hot in the Shade/VIP	$8
'92/Revenge	Triangle/various	KISS Revenge/Local Crew	$7
'92/Revenge	Square/various	KISS Revenge/After Show	$7
'92/Revenge	Rectangle/various	KISS Revenge/Support Act	$7
'92/Revenge	Rectangle/various	KISS Revenge/VIP	$8

Revenge satin passes were made in blue, green, orange, and red.

LAMINATED BACKSTAGE PASSES

Year/Tour	Description	Value
'76/Destroyer	Logo at top; "Summer Tour '76" on bottom; pass has room for the roadie's photograph	$18
'77–'78/Love Gun— Alive II	Says "KISS All World Tour 1977–1978" and has room for the roadie's photograph	$16
'87–'88/Crazy Nights	Back pass with yellow logo; says "Crazy Nights/1987–88 Tour"	$12

Year/Tour	Description	Value
'88/*Crazy Nights*/ Japan	White pass with illustration of band, black logo, and Japanese lettering	$16
'90/*Hot in the Shade*	Black pass with orange KISS logo and illustration of the Sphinx; "VIP" at bottom	$12
'92/*Revenge*/U.S. Club Tour	Black pass with red KISS logo and "Revenge/All Access"	$12
'92/*Revenge*/U.S. Arena Tour	Black pass with Statue of Liberty and KISS logo—All Access	$20
'92/*Revenge*/U.S. Arena Tour	Blue pass with Statue of Liberty and KISS logo—VIP	$12
'92/*Revenge*/U.S. Arena Tour	Yellow pass with Statue of Liberty and KISS logo—Support	$12

BOOTLEG BACKSTAGE PASSES

There are also many bootleg backstage passes, both satins and laminates. In general, passes that advertise one particular show or promoter are also considered bootleg passes. Very often bootleg passes are advertised as authentic passes, so look each pass over carefully before you consider buying it. Bootleg passes are generally only worth $.50–4, depending on the quality of the artwork.

EPHEMERA

BOOKS

KISS, by Robert Duncan (1978)
KISS biography including black-and-white photos and interviews with Paul, Gene, Ace, and Peter. $10–15

KISS (Headliners Series), by John Swenson (1978)
KISS biography from the popular Headliners series, which also had books on The Who and other artists. The KISS book includes many black-and-white photos from 1973–1977. $10–15

Rock Stars, by Scholastic Books (1979)
Geared toward the junior-high-age student, this book includes artists such as Fleetwood Mac and Billy Joel. The chapter on KISS is 15 pages long and full of errors, but there are a couple of good black-and-white photos. $5–7

Rock's Biggest Ten, by Scholastic Books (1979)
Another Scholastic compilation book, this one chronicling the 10 biggest rock stars of 1979; includes chapters on the Bee Gees, Peter Frampton, and KISS. The KISS chapter is 14 pages long, with 2 black-and-white photos. $5–7

KISS: The Real Story, by Peggy Tomarkin (1979)
This large softcover book tells the story of KISS from their humble beginnings to *Dynasty*. The photos, mostly black and white, are excellent, and the book includes many obscure facts and interesting events in KISStory. $30–35

KISS—Authentica Biografia Illustrada, by Joan Singla (1984)
64-page band biography written in Spanish. Published in Spain in 1984; 1977 band photo on cover. $25–30

KISS—Shout It Out, by Nick Seymour (1985)
Published in Sweden in 1985, this is a 72-page biography and discography of the band up to that time. Contains black-and-white pictures. $20–25

KISS, by Paolo Piccini (1987)
Published in Italy in 1987, this 100-page book is a brief history of KISS, with many color photos. $15–20

Still on Fire, by Dave Thomas and Anders Holm (1988)
This 1988 biography, published in England, is a pretty good biography of the band and contains many nice color photos. There are some inexplicable flaws (for example, Gene's real name is listed as Stein instead of Klein), but overall, it's a nice book to have. $20–25

U.S. TOURBOOKS

The tourbooks listed were sold on tour. Tourbooks were also sold through the KISS Army, and may vary slightly from the ones sold on tour. For example, Japanese fans who ordered the

U.S. *Love Gun* tourbook from the KISS Army Fan Club got a tourbook printed in Japanese, but otherwise exactly like the U.S. copy.

1) *Alive!* Tour
   24 pages
   11 by 11 inches
   Cover says, "KISS on Tour—1976." Cover photo is live shot from 1975. All photos in tourbook are from 1975. Mint, $60–70; Good, $40–50

2A) *Destroyer/Rock and Roll Over* Tour
   16 pages
   11 by 17 inches
   Cover says, "On Tour." Cover photo shows lit logo, smoky stage, and kids in crowd. All shots in the tourbook are from the *Destroyer* tour. Mint, $40–50; Good, $30–40

2B) *Destroyer/Rock and Roll Over* Tour
   16 pages
   11 by 17 inches

U.S. KISS tourbooks, 1976–1983

Exact same tourbook as above, except that every single Paul Stanley photo is different from 2A. Mint, $40–50; Good, $30–40

3) *Love Gun/Alive II* Tour
   20 pages
   11 by 17 inches
   Cover says, "World Tour '77 & '78." Cover has red logo and close-up photos of each member's face (Paul is holding a rose). Photos inside are from the Japanese *Rock and Roll Over* tour and the U.S. *Love Gun* tour. Inside back cover shows previous album covers. Back cover photo shows KISS in Japan, wearing kimonos. Mint, $35–45; Good, $25–35

4A) *Dynasty Tour*
   20 pages
   10 by 14 inches
   Cover shows black KISS logo on silver background, with the cover of the *Dynasty* LP beneath it. Inside front cover (page 2) is a posed shot on the *Dynasty* stage. Page facing that (page 3) is an ad for the Bally KISS Pinball Machine. Then each member has a 2-page spread with 1 picture of just his eyes, 3 small posed photos, and 1 full-page shot. The page opposite the inside back cover is an ad for the Paul Stanley Ibanez guitar. Mint, $30–35; Good, $25–30

U.S. KISS tourbooks, 1984–1990

4B) *Dynasty* Tour
20 pages
10 by 14 inches
Same cover as 4A. Page 2 (inside front cover) is the same as 4A, but page 3 is live shots of Gene, page 4 is live shots of Paul, and the pinball machine ad is on page 5. Each member's 2-page spread has the "eyes" picture, 6–8 small photos (some live, some posed), and the full-page shot. After Peter's pages, instead of the Paul Stanley ad, there is a Gene Simmons ad for Sunn Amplifiers. Following that is a page of live shots of Ace, then a page of live shots of Peter. Mint, $30–35; Good, $25–30

4C) *Dynasty* Tour
20 pages
10 by 14 inches
This tourbook is a combination of 4A and 4B, with the same cover. 4C has the live-photo pages like 4B, but each member's 2-page spread is the same as in 4A, with 1 "eyes" shot, 3 small posed photos, and 1 full-page shot. Ad page is for Paul Stanley Ibanez. Mint, $30–35; Good, $25–30

5) *Creatures* Tour
24 pages
11 by 14 inches
Cover says, "10th Anniversary Tour" and has an illustration of a tank on it. Everyone who had been a member of KISS up to that point (Gene, Paul, Ace, Peter, Eric Carr, Vinnie Vincent) has his own 2-page spread, and 1 section in the beginning of the tourbook shows KISS group photos from 1973 to 1982 (although the photo labeled "1978" is from 1979, and all the photos after that are off by 1 year). This was the last tourbook with makeup, and it is also the most rare U.S. tourbook, as it was only available on the later part of the tour. Mint, $90–100; Good, $65–70

6) *Lick It Up* Tour
24 pages
11 by 14 inches
Cover says, "World Tour 1984" and shows sepia-toned (brownish) photo of (left to right) VV/GS/PS/EC (no makeup). Photos inside are from 1983/1984. Mint, $30–35; Good, $25–30

7A) *Animalize* Tour
28 pages
9.5 by 12.5 inches
Cover says, "World Tour 1984–85" and shows (left to right) Gene, Eric Carr, Paul, and Mark St. John. Photos inside are from 1984, many from the *Heaven's On Fire* video. Mint, $20–25; Good, $15–20

7B) *Animalize* Tour
28 pages
9.5 by 12.5 inches
Cover says, "World Tour 1984–85" and shows (left to right) Bruce, Paul, Gene, and Eric Carr. Photos inside are from 1984, with all Mark photos

replaced by Bruce photos (except the shot of Mark's hand!), and many other photos in 7B are different than in 7A. Mint, $20–25; Good, $15–20

8) *Asylum* Tour
28 pages
11 by 14 inches
Front cover is the top half of the *Asylum* LP cover (Paul's and Gene's faces), and the back cover of the tourbook is the bottom half of the LP cover (Eric's and Bruce's faces). All photos inside are from 1985. Mint, $20–25; Good, $15–20

9) *Crazy Nights* Tour
24 pages
13 by 19.5 inches
Huge tourbook! Cover says, "Crazy Nights World Tour 1987–88" and has a black background and photos of each band member in the letters of the logo. All photos inside are from 1987, and the photography is great. There is also considerable background information on each member. Mint, $25–30; Good, $20–25

10) *Hot in the Shade* Tour
20 pages
13.25 by 19.5 inches
Another enormous tourbook. Cover shows the Sphinx in sunglasses with an orange KISS logo behind it, and the words "Hot in the Shade World Tour 1990–91" at the bottom. Photos inside are from 1990, both live and posed shots. There is also a section toward the end called "Great Moments in KISS-tory" which chronicles the important events in KISS's history from 1972 to 1990. Mint, $25–30; Good, $20–25

11) *Revenge* Tour
13.25 inches by 19.5 inches
Again, very large in size. Cover has band photo from the back cover of the CD and the word "Revenge" in red. Shots inside are live and posed shots from 1992.

FOREIGN TOURBOOKS

On the European *Destroyer* tour, the tourbooks sold were the U.S. *Alive!* tourbooks.

1) *Rock and Roll Over* Tour, Japan
40 pages
10 by 16.25 inches
Illustrated "Samurai" cover with red, yellow, and silver logo. Contains both color and black-and-white photos, writing is in Japanese, and there are 9 pages of advertisements. Mint, $90–100; Good, $65–70

  2) *Love Gun* Tour, Japan
      40 pages
      10 by 16.25 inches
      Cover shows 2 *Love Gun*–era photos; top photo is posed, bottom photo is live,
      and there are 2 blue KISS logos and 1 red KISS logo. Mostly black-and-white
      pages; some color pages. Printed in Japanese, with 9 pages of advertisements.
      Mint, $90–100; Good, $65–70
3A) *Unmasked* Tour, Europe
      32 pages
      9 by 12 inches
      Cover shows Gene, Paul, Ace, and Eric Carr onstage. (The photo was taken
      at the Palladium, Eric's first show, then was retouched later to reflect the change
      in Eric's makeup.) Full of color photos, including more "retouched" Palladium
      shots. The back covers of these tourbooks may have varied, depending on the
      country. Some of the tourbooks also contain a small paper advertisement for
      Attack of the Phantoms stapled into the centerfold. This European tour covered
      Italy, England, France, West Germany, the Netherlands, and Sweden. The
      German version of the tourbook contained German KISS logos, not standard
      ones. Mint, $70–80; Good, $55–60
3B) *Unmasked* Tour, Australia
      36 pages
      9 by 12 inches
      Same cover and photos as 3A, but with 4 pages of advertisements added.
      Back cover says, "Aussie Tour 1980." The 1980 Australian tour covered
      Australia and New Zealand. Mint, $70–80; Good, $55–60

Japanese tourbooks (1977, 1978, 1988)

Foreign tourbooks: Australian *Unmasked* tour, European *Lick It Up* tour, and the Donington Monsters of Rock tourbook from 1988

4) *Lick It Up* Tour, Europe
   24 pages
   11 by 14 inches
   Same cover as the U.S. *Creatures* tourbook (tank firing) with "World Tour 1983–1984" in orange letters on the bottom. All the photos are the same as in the U.S. *Lick It Up* tourbook, except the first 2 inside pages. (This tourbook has the album cover on 1 page, and a different photo of Paul on the next page). Mint, $40–45; Good, $30–35

(For the *Animalize* European tour, the tourbooks sold were the same as the first U.S. *Animalize* tourbook with Mark St. John).

5) Donington/Monsters of Rock Festival
   44 pages
   11.5 by 13.5 inches
   This tourbook is actually the program for an event held in England on August 20, 1988, at Castle Donington. It's a yearly event, but this was the only time KISS performed there. Of the 44 pages, there are 5 that contain information and photos of KISS, and there are 2 full-page KISS ads, 1 for the *KISS eXposed* videotape, and 1 for the U.K. leg of the *Crazy Nights* tour. Mint, $15–20; Good, $10–15

COMIC BOOKS

MARVEL KISS COMICS

KISS Marvel Comic #1, 1977
Printed in real KISS blood! (Actual vials of blood from the band members were added to the red dye when the comic book was printed.) An oversize comic book, it included a small poster in the middle of the book as well as articles on how the idea of a KISS comic book came about. Written by Steve Gerber and Michael Gross, *KISS Marvel Comic #1* tells the story of KISS versus Dr. Doom! $25–35

KISS Marvel Comic #2, 1978
In the sequel to the original KISS comic book, KISS fights a villain named Khalis-Wu to save the land of Khyscz . . . pronounced "KISS," of course! The poster in the center is an illustration of KISS with a light blue background. $20–30

HOWARD THE DUCK COMICS

Howard the Duck, Volume 1, #12; 1977
This issue of *Howard the Duck* (a comic-book duck from another planet) tells of a girl, Winda, who believes she is possessed. In the last panel of this issue, Winda has the demons exorcised from her. . . . They are, of course, Gene, Paul, Ace, and Peter. $6–8

Howard the Duck, Volume 1, #13; 1977
Continuing the story from the previous issue, KISS tells Howard that when he meets Reality head-on, he should "KISS it, smack in the face." Then they go back into Winda's brain and disappear. $6–8

BOOTLEG KISS COMICS

Rock and Roll Comics: KISS, 1990
Put out by Revolutionary Comics, Rock and Roll Comics covered artists such as Bon Jovi and Guns & Roses. The KISS issue traces the band's history up to the release of *Hot in the Shade*. This comic book started a flood of other bootleg KISS comic books, most of which contain numerous mistakes and very poor artwork. 1st pressing, $10; 2nd pressing, $5

Other bootleg KISS comic books made in the 1990s (such as *Rock Fantasy Comics* and *Personality Comics*) are generally worth about $2–5, depending on the quality of the artwork.

SONGBOOKS AND SHEET MUSIC

SONGBOOKS

Values (assuming Mint/EX condition):

Title	Value	Title	Value
Destroyer	$20–25	Dynasty	$20–25
The Originals	$40–50	Unmasked	$20–25
Rock and Roll Over	$20–25	Crazy Nights	$12–15
Love Gun	$20–25	KISS E-Z Guitar (green cover)	$25
Alive II	$30–35		
Double Platinum	$20–25	KISS E-Z Guitar (red cover)	$25
Paul Stanley (solo LP)	$20		
Gene Simmons (solo LP)	$20	KISS Rock Charts (with masks)	$30
Ace Frehley (solo LP)	$20		
Peter Criss (solo LP)	$20	Almo Rapid Play Series	$25

SHEET MUSIC

Years	Value
1973–1978 (such as "Hard Luck Woman")	$15–18
1979–1983 (such as "I Was Made for Lovin' You")	$12–15
1984–1992 (such as "Forever")	$10–12

MAGAZINES

<u>ALL-KISS MAGAZINES</u>

<u>Special Title</u>	<u>Date</u>	<u>Volume/ Issue #</u>	<u>Original Price</u>	<u>Value</u>	<u>Notes</u>
Music Life Magazine (Japan) ("KISS Encyclopedia," red cover)	5/77		$12	$25	Photos and info (in Japanese) about KISS's first Japanese tour ('77). Large poster included
Creem Special Edition—KISS	Fall '77		$2	$25	First live photos with Love Gun outfits; also, vintage photos from 1974 to 1976.
Music Life Magazine (Japan) ("KISS Special," black cover)	5/78		$12	$25	Same as Music Life above, but for 1978 Japanese tour.
Teen Machine Presents KISS	5/78	Vol. 1, #1	$1	$10	Many pinups plus group centerfold.
Grooves Mag. Presents KISS	1978	Vol. 1, #1	$2	$15	Contains 2-by-3-foot color poster, stories, photos
Grooves Presents KISS II	6/78	Vol. 1, #3	$1.95	$15	Came with "life-size" poster.
Grooves Presents KISS	10/78	Vol. 1, #7	$1.95	$15	Came with 16-month calendar ('78–'79).
KISS Meets the Phantom	10/78		$2.50	$25	Has interviews and photos from the movie.
TV Superstar—KISS Pinup Book	10/78	Vol. 3, #1	$1	$10	Pinups ('74–'77) and group centerfold.

cont.

Special Title	Date	Volume/ Issue #	Original Price	Value	Notes
SuperTeen Special—Take an Inside Look at KISS	11/78	#1	$1	$10	Stories about each member, plus 6 color pinups and a group poster.
Teen Favorites Presents KISS	1978		$1.50	$10	Early photos and centerfold (Japan '77 shot).
Punk Rock Special—KISS	1978	Vol. 1, #2	$1.50	$10	8 color pinups ('75–'77) and articles.
Teen Star Special Issue—KISS	1978		$1.50	$10	Magazine folds out into 2 posters. Group shot on cover.
Teen Star Special Issue—KISS	1978	#2	$1.50	$10	Magazine folds out into 2 posters. Paul on cover.
KISS Krazy (TV Superstar)	4/79	Vol. 3, #4	$1.25	$10	Included 10 color pinups.
The Best of KISS #2	1979		$2.50	$10	Lots of pinups and group centerfold poster.
Paul Stanley— Groupie Rock Special	1979	Vol. 1, #6	$1.95	$10	Photos from '74–'78. There are also Gene, Ace, and Peter issues in this series.
Gene Simmons— KISS Collection Series	1979	Vol. 2, #3	$1.95	$10	There are also Paul, Ace, and Peter issues in this series.
Official KISS Poster Book	1979	Winter #4	$2.50	$20	Came with four 2-sided posters (b&w 1 side, color other side). Plus live Dynasty shots.

Special Title	Date	Volume/ Issue #	Original Price	Value	Notes
KISS Special	1979	Spring	$1.95	$8	KISS articles and b&w photos.
KISSMania—TV Superstar	12/79	Vol. 2, #2	$1.25	$8	*Dynasty* pinups and centerfold (group '79/ GS '78).
The Brand New KISS—Teen Talk #2	1980		$1.50	$10	Centerfold of KISS at Palladium (NY 1980).
KISS Fever—TV Superstar	8/80	Vol. 6, #4	$1.25	$8	Mostly all KISS; *Dynasty* pinups. Some other artists featured (Rex Smith, Village People).
KISS Strikes Back— Teen Machine	1/81	Vol. 3, #4	$1.50	$8	Pinups plus first shots of Eric Carr and some Palladium photos.
Starline presents KISS	1987	Vol. 2, #1	$3.95 Can. $4.50	$10	Discography and video-graphy, and several fold-out posters with and without makeup.
Movie Mirror presents KISS Photo Album	1/87	Vol. 31, #2	$2.50 Can. $2.75 U.K. £1.45	$8	Mostly KISS, but some articles about other artists. Includes color pin-ups and several KISS articles.
KISS eXposed—The Official Magazine —Rock Scene Spot-lights #2	7/87	Vol. 1, #2	$3.95 Can. $4.50	$15	Came out when the *eXposed* video was released. Contains photos from *eXposed*, plus 2-sided poster (PS '82/GS '77).

cont.

Special Title	Date	Volume/Issue #	Original Price	Value	Notes
Creem Collectors Series	12/87	Vol. 2, #1	$2.95 Can. $3.50	$15	Complete history of band and discography. Incl: 2-sided poster (*Crazy Nights* photo/*Dynasty* photo).
The KISS Tours 1974–1988— Rock Scene Spotlights #5	9/88		$3.95 Can. $4.50	$10	Photos and set lists from the tours, plus 2-sided poster (group live '86/ posed '82).
The KISS Kollection —Teen Throb	4/89	Vol. 2, #1	$3.50 Can. $3.95	$10	Color photos from different years, plus group centerfold from Empire State Bldg. session.
KISS Guitarists— Rock Scene Spotlights #9	9/89		$3.95 Can. $4.50	$10	Talks to all guitarists in KISS history about equipment, also 2-sided poster (GS/PS '82).
Metal Madness— The Might and Magic of KISS	11/89	Vol. 1, #3	$2.95 Can. $3.50	$10	Contained pull-out poster of KISS through the years (with and without makeup).
KISS on the Record—Rock Scene Spotlights #11	2/90		$3.95 Can. $4.50	$10	Interviews with all 4 about all of KISS's LPs; came with 2-sided poster (makeup shots).
Rip Photo Special	6/90	Vol. 2, #4	$2.95 Can. $3.50	$10	Photos of band from '75 to '90, plus large poster of band ('76 Christmas shot).
KISS—the Videos —Rock Scene Spotlights #15	7/90		$3.95 Can. $4.50	$10	Complete guide to KISS's videos up to *Rise To It*, plus pull-out poster of PS/ GS/AF/PC.

Special Title	Date	Volume/ Issue #	Original Price	Value	Notes
KISS Alive 1990— H.I.T.S. Tour—Rock Scene Spotlights #19	1/91		$3.95 Can. $4.50	$10	Contained 1990 tour photos and 2-sided poster (1981 group shot/1990 Paul shot).
The KISS Kollection —Rock Scene Spotlights #22	5/91		$3.95 Can. $4.50	$10	Interviews with all 4 and 2-sided poster (H.I.T.S. collage/Paul live shot, '76).
Metal Muscle Presents a Tribute to KISS	10/92		$3.50 Can. $3.95	$10	3 Giant pull-out posters and a tribute to Eric Carr.

OTHER MAGAZINES

Magazine	Date	Volume/ Issue #	Original Price	Value	Notes
Rock Scene	9/75	Vol. 3, #5	$.75	$15	First U.S. magazine to have KISS on cover.
Circus	4/8/76	#130	$1.00	$10	First time on cover of Circus (Destroyer outfits); the article deals with the making of Destroyer.
Creem	7/76	Vol. 8, #2	$1.00	$10	First time on cover of Creem (U.S. Tour '76 pose); with centerfold poster (same pose).

cont.

Magazine	Date	Volume/ Issue #	Original Price	Value	Notes
Hit Parader	7/76	Vol. 35, #144	$.75	$10	First time on cover of HP ('75 posed shot); the article covers the band's history to that point.
Creem	1/77	Vol. 8, #8	$1.00	$10	Band on cover (Christmas shot with robes); plus centerfold of band in snow (same session).
Hit Parader	3/77		$.75	$10	Group on cover, *Destroyer* outfits.
Creem	8/77	Vol. 8, #2	$1.00	$10	Illus. cover of band as 4-headed monster over Tokyo; article deals with Japan tour.
Circus	8/4/77	#161	$1.00	$9	Paul on cover. Article about making of *Love Gun*.
Song Hits	12/77	Vol. 41, #142	$.50	$5	Cover is posed *Love Gun* group shot.
Circus	12/22/77	#171	$1.00	$9	Gene on cover; article about *Alive II*.
Circus	4/13/78	#179	$1.00	$9	Peter on cover; *Love Gun* outfit. Article is about Peter's opinions on music, movies, etc.
Hit Parader	5/78	Vol. 37, #166	$1.00	$9	Gene on cover (*Love Gun* outfit) with red tube.

Magazine	Date	Volume/ Issue #	Original Price	Value	Notes
Rock Scene	9/78	Vol. 6, #6	$1.00	$10	Cover of band from 2nd Japanese tour.
Guitar Player	1/79	Vol.13, #1	$1.50	$10	Ace on cover. Interviews with PS/ GS/AF about technical stuff.
Hit Parader	2/79	Vol. 38, #175	$1.00	$9	Gene on cover (*Love Gun* outfit); PC centerfold.
Hit Parader	6/79	Vol. 38, #179	$1.00	$9	Paul on cover.
Hit Parader	11/79	Vol. 38, #184	$1.00	$9	Ace on cover (*Dynasty* outfit).
People Magazine	8/18/80	Vol. 14, #7	$.75	$12	1st national publication with Eric Carr. Band on cover with Eric's old makeup.
Circus— Special 11th Anniversary Issue	10/28/80	#248	$1.50	$12	1st time band was on cover of *Circus* with Eric Carr, but last time on cover of *Circus* with makeup.
Hit Parader	1/82		$1.00	$10	Paul on cover (*The Elder* shot); last time on cover of HP with makeup.
Kerrang!	7/29/82	#21		$13	Close-up shot of Gene on cover; article talks about new KISS LP, *Creatures of the Night*.

cont.

Magazine	Date	Volume/ Issue #	Original Price	Value	Notes
Kerrang!	4/5/83	#41		$13	Cover shot of Gene spitting blood (*Creatures of the Night* tour) and review and photos from *Creatures of the Night* concert.
Kerrang!	10/20/83	#53		$13	Cover shows illustration of Paul covering his face; article talks about unmasking and *Lick It Up*.
BURRN	5/86			$12	Japanese magazine; Gene on cover.
Kerrang!	9/17/87	#155		$10	Band photo on cover; article talks about new LP, *Crazy Nights*.
Faces	10/87	Vol. 4, #9	$2.50 $2.75 Can.	$5	GS/PS on cover. Interview with Paul and centerfold of group.
Rip	10/87	Vol. 1, #11	$2.50 $2.95 Can.	$5	GS/PS on cover. Group centerfold (*Crazy Nights*–era shot). Article about *Crazy Nights* LP.
BURRN	10/87			$12	Japanese magazine; Paul on cover.
Rock Scene	12/87	Vol. 12, #12	$2.95 $3.50 Can.	$5	*Crazy Nights* photo of band on cover; inside, Paul talks about the new LP (*Crazy Nights*).

Magazine	Date	Volume/ Issue #	Original Price	Value	Notes
Kerrang!	1/30/88	#172		$8	Live shot of Paul on cover; review of *Crazy Nights* concert.
Song Hits	4/89	Vol. 53, #268	$1.95 $2.25 Can.	$5	Cover is group photo from *Smashes, Thrashes and Hits* era.
Kerrang!	8/12/89	#251		$8	Posed band shot on cover; article about studio work for *Hot in the Shade*.
Rip	6/90	Vol. 4, #7	$2.95 $3.50 Can.	$6	Gene and Paul from *Rise To It* video on cover (with makeup); band centerfold (without).
Kerrang!	2/1/92	#317		$8	First magazine with Gene's "new look" and photos of *Revenge* lineup; Gene on cover.
Raw	2/5/92	#90		$8	Gene on cover; article has Gene reviewing all of KISS's albums up to *Revenge*.
Livewire	7/92	Vol. 2, #7	$2.95 $3.50 Can.	$5	*Revenge* photo of band on cover; article talks about new CD (*Revenge*).
Guitar School	7/92	Vol. 4, #4	$3.50 $3.95 Can.	$8	Cover shot of Gene from 1978; article talks about new CD and technical guitar stuff.

cont.

Magazine	Date	Volume/ Issue #	Original Price	Value	Notes
Circus	7/31/92		$3.50	$5	Paul/Gene on cover; article about *Revenge*.
Hit Parader	8/92		$3.50	$7	Issue came with 16-page mini-booklet; "HP Salutes 20 Years of KISS." GS/PS on cover.

FANZINES AND KISS ARMY KITS

The KISS Army, KISS's official fan club, started publishing newsletters in early 1976, and stopped in 1981. During those 5 years, they printed and mailed many newsletters, KISS Army folders, order forms, and other cool printed material. Here are some of the things put out by the KISS Army, and their values today:

KISS Army folders—Some had the KISS Army logo; others had that logo in front of an explosion in space. Folders themselves are worth $3–4, but if they are complete with photos, newsletters, and order forms, they are worth up to $25.

KISS Army newsletters—These are worth $6–10 each, depending on condition and significance of the issue. (For example, the first KISS Army newsletter, Volume 1, Number 1, or the issue introducing Eric Carr as the new drummer, are worth more than some of the other issues.)

Biographies—1st one was printed on gold paper and had a short story about each member, along with his astrological sign; value—$2; second discography was larger, on brown paper, and had "Classified Information" written in red, pictures of the 4 solo-LP covers, and information about each member. $4

1978 KISS discography—Printed on yellow paper, this discography covered all of KISS's albums up to the solo LPs, showing photos of the covers and listing the songs on each album. $3

Membership card and membership certificate—Card had KISS Army logo on one side; certificate also had KISS Army logo at top. $1 each

KISS Army color or black-and-white 8-by-10s—Printed on card stock, these photos were part of the KISS Army kits. $5–7 each

KISS Alive II *Card*—This was a folded piece of card stock with a 1977 live photo on both sides, presumably to be used like a greeting card. $8

KISS Army stamps—These stickers, the moisten-and-stick type, came in a perforated set of 6 (1 shot of each member, 1 sticker with all 4 photos, and 1 with the KISS Army "explosion" logo). $10

KISS Army merchandise order forms—Various styles. $2–4 each

Sadly, the official KISS Army disbanded in 1981, but many unofficial fanzines were started to take up the slack. Unfortunately, most of them go out of business before their 2nd birthday. Unofficial KISS fanzines are worth anywhere from $.50 to $8, depending on the quality of the newsletter.

KISS Army kits/newsletters (See "Magazines")

KISS backpack—Sealed, in package, $75; without packaging, $60

KISS beach towel—Towel A (illustration of 1977 shot of band on Plexiglas cubes, with red and blue logo at bottom, copyright 1979, $60; Towel B (red and blue logo at top, and head-and-shoulders illustration of each member, *Love Gun* era), $60

KISS bedspread—Sealed, in package, $140; without packaging, $120

KISS belt buckles (see "Jewelry, Pins, and Patches")

KISS bubble gum cards—1st Series, complete set (numbers 1–66), $25–30; 1st Series, single package with wrapper, sealed, $2; 2nd Series, complete set (numbers 67–132), $25–30; 2nd Series, single package with wrapper, sealed, $2; 1st or 2nd Series, individual cards, $.50 each
1st Series, Revised (Australian series with Eric Carr)—1st Series, Revised, complete set (numbers 1–66, $40–50; 1st Series, Revised, single package with wrapper, sealed, $7; 1st Series, Revised, individual cards (GS, PS, AF), $1 each; 1st Series, Revised, individual cards (EC or group), $3–4 each

KISS Chu-Bops (record-shaped bubble gum in cardboard "LP cover")—*Dynasty*, sealed, $15; *Dynasty*, open, with gum, $8–10; *Dynasty*, cover only, $7; *Unmasked*, sealed, $8; *Unmasked*, open, with gum, $4–6; *Unmasked*, cover only, $3

KISS clothing—Any piece of *official* KISS clothing from Monsanto (circa 1978): Mint/EX condition, $175–225

KISS colorforms—Mint condition, complete, $35; Good/fair condition, or incomplete, $15–20

KISS cups (from Majik Market)—Set of 8 cups, $150

KISS curtains—Sealed, in package, $140; without packaging, $120

KISS dolls (Paul, Gene, Ace, Peter)—Mint condition, in original boxes, $85 each, $350/set; Mint condition, without boxes, $55 each, $250/set; Very good/good condition, without boxes, $30 each, $125/set; Fair/poor condition, without boxes, $10–15 each, $50/set

KISS "On Tour" game—Sealed, $60; Mint, not sealed, complete, $50; Good condition, complete, $35; Fair/poor or incomplete, $15

KISS garbage can (wastebasket)—Mint condition, $75; Good/fair condition, $40

KISS gold coin (Made in Australia; available by mail order in U.S., circa 1980)—Mint, $20

KISS toy guitar (black or white plastic guitar with 1976 photo pasted on it)—1st or 2nd version, sealed in package, $125; 1st or 2nd version, mint but no package, $80; 1st or 2nd version, good/fair condition, $50

KISS Halloween costumes—Gene, Paul, Ace, or Peter: each, mint with box, $55; Gene, Paul, Ace, or Peter: each, good/fair with box, $40–45; Gene, Paul,

Ace, or Peter: each, no box, $15–20; Set of 4, mint with boxes, $225; Set of 4, good/fair with boxes, $180; Set of 4, no boxes, $75

KISS jackets—1st jacket (yellow/orange/purple with "flames"), mint, $110; 1st jacket (yellow/orange/purple with "flames"), good/fair, $90; 2nd jacket (red/white/black), mint, $110; 2nd jacket (red/white/black), good/fair, $90; Satin jacket (with tank design), mint, $60

(For *Animalize* satin jacket, see "Other Merchandise, 1984–1993.")

KISS "Dynasty" key chain—$15

KISS lunch box—Mint condition, with thermos, $75; Mint condition, no thermos, $50; Good condition, with thermos, $45; Good condition, no thermos, $30; Thermos alone, $10–20

KISS makeup kits—There are 2 different makeup kits. The 2nd one has a red and orange splash that says, "New Water-Soluble Formula," and there is a different ingredient list. Also, on the 2nd box, the weights of the makeup are listed, and the makeup is listed as "easily removable water-soluble makeup" instead of "easily removable professional stage makeup." The serial number on the first kit is #737–0201, and the serial number on the second kit is #739–0201. 1st or 2nd kit, sealed, $80; 1st or 2nd kit, mint/EX but open, makeup unused, $65–70; 1st or 2nd kit, good/fair condition, makeup used, $30–40

KISS Mardi Gras coins—1979 coin, silver or red, $5; 1983 *Creatures* coin, silver, $10

KISS microphone—Mint, with box, $50; Mint, no box, $35; "In Concert" set with microphone, mike stand, and amp, with box, $120; "In Concert" set, no box, $75

KISS mirrors—*Love Gun* mirror, 12 by 12 inches, $25; *Destroyer* mirror, 12 by 12 inches, $25; Bootleg mirrors, large (12 by 12 inches), $3–6; Bootleg mirrors, small (6 by 6 inches), $2–5

(For *Animalize* mirror, see "Other Merchandise, 1984–1993.")

KISS model van (*not* the remote-control van)—Sealed, $50; Mint, in box, open, $40–45; Incomplete or assembled, with box, $20; Incomplete or assembled, no box, $5–10

KISS notebooks—Paul Stanley, $15; Gene Simmons, $15; Ace Frehley, $15; Peter Criss, $15; Group (solo-LP artwork), $15; Group (live, *Alive II*), $20; Group (1978 posed shot), $20; Group (1979 posed individual shots), $20

KISS pencils (sold as a set of 4)—Set of 4 pencils, sealed, $20; Set of 4 pencils, no package, $12–15; Individual pencils, each, $3

KISS pens—There were 4 pens, one of each member (PS/GS/AF/PC), sold separately. Pen, still sealed (blister pack), each, $15; Pen, no packaging, each, $8–10; Pens, set of 4, still sealed, $70; Pens, set of 4, no packaging, $45

KISS pinball machine by Bally—Unassembled, in box, $1,200; Mint condition, assembled but virtually unplayed, $1,000; Excellent/very good condition, assembled/working, $750–850; Good/fair condition, assembled/working, $500–650; Poor condition, parts/lights missing, or not working, $200–250

KISS poster art—Sealed, with pens, $65; Open, mint condition, unused and complete, $50; Incomplete or used (colored in), $10–12

KISS poster put-ons (large stickers)—*Love Gun* (LP cover), mint/sealed, $8–10; *Alive II* (LP cover), mint/sealed, $8–10; U.S. Tour '76 (same as poster), mint/sealed, $8–10; Set of 3, mint/sealed, $30

KISS puffy stickers ("Rockstics")—Gene, Paul, Ace, or Peter: each, sealed, $10; Set of 4, sealed, $45

KISS puzzles—There are 6 KISS puzzles: 1 each of Paul, Gene, Ace, and Peter; one *Destroyer* cover art puzzle, and 1 of the *Love Gun* cover art. The individual puzzles were manufactured by Milton Bradley, and the cover art puzzles were made by APC (American Publishing Corp.). The Milton Bradley puzzles were sealed with glue (the paper that showed the puzzle picture came down low enough to be glued to the bottom of the box), but the APC puzzles were shrink-wrapped. Individual-member puzzles, sealed, each, $20–25; Individual-member puzzles, open but complete, each, $12–15; Individual-member puzzles, open but complete, set of 4, $75; *Destroyer* or *Love Gun* puzzle, sealed, $25–30; *Destroyer* or *Love Gun* puzzle, open but complete, $15–20 each

KISS radio (either white or black plastic transistor radio with KISS sticker)—Mint, with box, $60; Mint, no box, $45; Good/fair condition, no box, $25–35

KISS record player—Mint condition with box, $200; VG/good condition without box, $140

KISS remote control van—Mint, with box, $75; Good condition, no box, $50; Not in working order, $25

KISS rub & play set—Complete, unused, $30; Incomplete/used, $10–12

KISS shoelaces—With just KISS logos, mint condition, $12–15; With logos and faces, mint condition, $12–15

KISS showbeam cartridge—With box, $20; Without box, $12–15

KISS sleeping bag—Sealed, in package, $150; Without packaging, $125

KISS sponge—"KISS Army" sponge from *Dynasty* tour, mint, $20

KISS viewmaster reels—Set, sealed, $15; Set, with packaging but open, $6–8; Set of 3, sealed (KISS plus 2 others in blister pack), $20

KISS viewmaster double-vue cartridge—Sealed on cardboard, $40; Without packaging, $20

OTHER MERCHANDISE, 1984–1993

Animalize *bumper sticker*—Cover art, $3–5

Animalize *key chain*—Cover art, $2–4

Animalize *mirror*—Back cover group photo: 6 by 6 inches, $8–10

Animalize *satin jacket*—Woman's fingers "ripping" through logo, $30–35

Animalize *satin vest*—Same design as jacket, but vest style, $30–35

Crazy Nights *key chain*—Back cover art, $2–4

KISS logo necklace—Silver, sold on *Revenge* tour, $8

KISS sunglasses—Black with small KISS logos on arms; sold on *Hot in the Shade* tour, $8–10

KISS underwear—Black with pink print; sold on *Hot in the Shade* tour, $8–10

KISS underwear—Black with red print; sold on *Revenge* tour, $10

KISS condoms—White "matchbook" cover with purple KISS logo and two condoms inside, $5

PICKS AND STICKS

All collectible KISS picks have the name of the guitarist on 1 side and the KISS logo on the other. Picks can be white, yellow, red, black, or even pink; ink colors are black or gold. Unless specified otherwise, the band member's name is his autograph, not just a printed name.

Paul Stanley and Gene Simmons picks (from KISS tours):
    White with black (1973–1983). $12–15
    Yellow with black (1983–1986). $8–10
    Pink with black, red with gold, and black with gold (1985–1986). $7–10
    White with gold (1985–1990). $5–8
Ace Frehley picks (when he was with KISS):
    White with black, name printed block style (1976–1978). $12–15
    White with black, autograph printed (1979–1980). $12–15
Vinnie Vincent picks (when he was with KISS):
    White with black (1982–1983). $10–12
    Yellow with black (1983–1984). $8–10
Bruce Kulick picks (from KISS tours):
    Pink/gold, black/gold, red/black (1985–1986). $7–10
    White with gold ink (1985–1990). $5–8
    White with black (1992). $5–8
    Yellow with black ink (1992) $5–8
Paul Stanley picks (from his 1989 solo tour):
    White picks with gold ink, Paul's signature, but no KISS logo. $12–15

Peter Criss always used natural-wood drumsticks. Eric Carr usually used wooden drumsticks that were painted white, but he was also known to use woodgrain, fluorescent orange, or fluorescent green sticks on occasion. Eric Singer's sticks are natural wood.

Peter Criss (printed name, logo; black ink). $40 per stick
Eric Carr (autograph, logo; silver ink). $40 per stick
Eric Singer (autograph, logo; purple ink). $25 per stick

AUTOGRAPHED ITEMS

It's often difficult to determine whether an autograph is real. Many people can do a convincing forgery of an autograph they've seen before, and KISS's autographs are commonly seen in old magazines, on some KISS merchandise, and on the inside cover of *Alive!*. Unless you have some verification that the autograph is real (such as a photo of the band member signing the item), don't spend a lot of money on an autographed item.

If you do have some verification, or you absolutely trust the seller of the item, you should generally figure that the item is worth its own value plus ten dollars per autograph (i.e., an album that's usually worth $15, if autographed by Paul and Gene, would be worth $25). However, an item autographed by a band member who wasn't in the band when the item was released is worthless (i.e., a copy of *Love Gun* autographed by Eric Singer). It's always best to try to get the autograph yourself, anyway . . . then it has sentimental value, and that can't be measured!

RECORD AWARDS AND ONE-OF-A-KIND/RARE ITEMS

RECORD AWARDS

In the United States, gold awards are given for sales of 500,000 units; platinum awards are given for sales of 1,000,000 units. In Australia, gold awards are given for $500,000 in sales; platinum awards are given for $1,000,000 in sales. Other countries have still other requirements for gold or platinum awards.

But regardless of how the awards are figured, gold and platinum awards mean that a band has done well, and the awards are great collector's items. There are awards for albums, 45s, CDs, cassettes, videos, even 8-Track tapes. Many of the countries that produce KISS albums have given KISS gold and/or platinum awards, although the awards listed may not all exist from every one of the places listed.

Item	Award	Where From	Value
LP (*KISS* and *Creatures of the Night*)	Gold	U.S.A.	$500
LP (*KISS* and *Creatures of the Night*)	Platinum	U.S.A.	$600
LP (*Lick It Up* and *Hot in the Shade*)	Gold	U.S.A.	$300
LP (*Lick It Up* and *Hot in the Shade*)	Platinum	U.S.A.	$400
45 ("I Was Made . . .")	Gold	U.S.A.	$300
8-Track tape	Gold	U.S.A.	$250
8-Track tape	Platinum	U.S.A.	$350
CD/Cassette/(LP)	Gold	U.S.A.	$300
CD/Cassette/(LP)	Platinum	U.S.A.	$400
Cassette only	Gold	U.S.A.	$200
Cassette only	Platinum	U.S.A.	$300
Videotape	Gold	U.S.A.	$250
Videotape	Platinum	U.S.A.	$350
LP (*KISS* to *Creatures of the Night*)	Gold	Canada or Europe	$450
LP (*KISS* to *Creatures of the Night*)	Platinum	Canada or Europe	$550
LP (*Lick It Up* to *Revenge*)	Gold	Canada or Europe	$250
LP (*Lick It Up* to *Revenge*)	Platinum	Canada or Europe	$350
45 (1973–1983)	Gold	Canada or Europe	$250
45 (1984–1993)	Gold	Canada or Europe	$200
8-Track tape	Gold	Canada or Europe	$200
CD/Cassette/LP	Gold	Canada or Europe	$250
CD/Cassette/LP	Platinum	Canada or Europe	$350
Cassette only	Gold	Canada or Europe	$150
Cassette only	Platinum	Canada or Europe	$250
Cassette single	Gold	Canada or Europe	$150
Videotape	Gold	Canada or Europe	$200

Item	Award	Where From	Value
Videotape	Platinum	Canada or Europe	$300
LP (*KISS* to *Creatures of the Night*)	Gold	Australia/New Zealand	$450
LP (*KISS* to *Creatures of the Night*)	Platinum	Australia/New Zealand	$550
LP (*Lick It Up* to *Revenge*)	Gold	Australia/New Zealand	$250
LP (*Lick It Up* to *Revenge*)	Platinum	Australia/New Zealand	$350
45 (1973–1983)	Gold	Australia/New Zealand	$250
45 (1984–1993)	Gold	Australia/New Zealand	$200
8-Track tape	Gold	Australia/New Zealand	$200
CD/Cassette/LP	Gold	Australia/New Zealand	$250
CD/Cassette/LP	Platinum	Australia/New Zealand	$350
Cassette only	Gold	Australia/New Zealand	$150
Cassette only	Platinum	Australia/New Zealand	$250
Videotape	Gold	Australia/New Zealand	$200
Videotape	Platinum	Australia/New Zealand	$300
LP (*KISS* to *Creatures of the Night*)	Gold	Japan/Asia	$600
LP (*KISS* to *Creatures of the Night*)	Platinum	Japan/Asia	$700
LP (*Lick It Up* or later)	Gold	Japan/Asia	$400
LP (*Lick It Up* or later)	Platinum	Japan/Asia	$500
45 (1973–1983)	Gold	Japan/Asia	$350
45 (1984 or later)	Gold	Japan/Asia	$400
8-Track tape	Gold	Japan/Asia	$350
CD	Gold	Japan/Asia	$400
CD	Platinum	Japan/Asia	$500
Cassette	Gold	Japan/Asia	$300
Cassette	Platinum	Japan/Asia	$400
Cassette single	Gold	Japan/Asia	$200
Videotape	Gold	Japan/Asia	$350
Videotape	Platinum	Japan/Asia	$450
LP (*KISS* to *Creatures of the Night*)	Gold	Mexico/South America	$450
LP (*KISS* to *Creatures of the Night*)	Platinum	Mexico/South America	$500
LP (*Lick It Up* to *Revenge*)	Gold	Mexico/South America	$250
LP (*Lick It Up* to *Revenge*)	Platinum	Mexico/South America	$350
45 (1973–1983)	Gold	Mexico/South America	$250
45 (1984–1993)	Gold	Mexico/South America	$200
8-Track tape	Gold	Mexico/South America	$200
CD/Cassette/LP	Gold	Mexico/South America	$250

Item	Award	Where From	Value
CD/Cassette/LP	Platinum	Mexico/South America	$350
Cassette only	Gold	Mexico/South America	$150
Cassette only	Platinum	Mexico/South America	$250
Cassette single	Gold	Mexico/South America	$150
Videotape	Gold	Mexico/South America	$200
Videotape	Platinum	Mexico/South America	$300

RARE ITEMS

One-of-a-kind items would include pieces of the band's clothing, personal items that band members gave away or donated to auctions, original pieces of artwork later used by KISS, or anything else that was an important part of KISStory that is now in the hands of a collector. Rare items include things that were made in small quantity, whether for sale or use by the band, that are seldom seen for sale. It would be impossible to list all the one-of-a-kind and rare KISS items that exist, but here are some items and, in cases where it is feasible, their approximate values:

Clothing that belonged to a member of KISS is very difficult to prove. Generally, if you didn't get it directly from the KISS member or from a legitimate auction of rock memorabilia (most of these provide certificates of authenticity), then there is no way to prove that it is not a handmade copy of the clothing worn by KISS. If the piece is legitimate, the value would depend on whose it was (something of Paul's or Gene's would be more valuable than something that belonged to Peter Criss or Vinnie Vincent) and what the item was (a belt would be worth less than a jacket). Age would also make a difference, and part of a KISS costume from the makeup days would be worth more than an item of personal clothing that was not part of a costume, but again, without proof of authenticity, items like that are pretty much worthless.

Paul Stanley firehouse hats—These were made in red, black, white, and yellow; Paul occasionally threw them out to the crowd, and they're very valuable. But there have also been fakes sold for large amounts of money, so be very careful. Used when Paul would sing "Firehouse," these fire hats were made from the real thing. A sticker was placed on the leather panel on the front of the hat. In the earlier years, the sticker had a large number 3, the KISS logo, and the word "Firehouse." These were made in both black and red. After the *Love Gun* tour, the sticker was changed to a KISS logo and Paul's signature, and the hats were either white, yellow, or red. (Some of the black hats Paul used in '75/'76 had no sticker, but it would be hard to prove that a hat with no sticker was actually one used by Paul.)

    1st type (with #3). $250–275

    2nd type (with name). $225–250

KISS motorcycle (Honda "Hawk") aka the "Honda KISSmobile"—Yes, there was an actual KISS motorcycle. Made by Honda in 1978, it was a Honda Hawk painted with KISS logos, the words "Honda KISSmobile," and the names of the 4 original members. Very, very rare!

Road Crew clothing—This would include any T-shirts, sweatshirts, or jackets specifically made for KISS's road crew. They usually have the KISS logo, the words "Road Crew," and sometimes the tour (year or album name). As always, beware of fakes. Older ones (earlier tours) would be worth more than ones from recent tours. In general, the T-shirts would be worth about $25–50, the sweatshirts $50–75, and the jackets $100–150.

Instruments—In 1980 Ibanez released copies of the Paul Stanley PS-10 ("Iceman") guitar to the general public. A very small number of that model were reissued in 1992. Also in 1980, Kramer guitars issued the Gene Simmons Bass Axe for sale to the public. In 1992 Gene developed a bass guitar called "The Punisher" for the B.C. Rich guitar company. These are the only 3 KISS guitars released for sale to the general public.

Band instruments—Although the Paul Stanley Ibanez Iceman and the Gene Simmons Bass Axe are valuable, any guitars actually used by members of KISS are worth even more. Again, this is something that is very hard to prove unless the guitar was custom-made for KISS, and/or you have a certificate of authenticity, but actual guitars (or parts of drum kits) used by KISS members are rare and valuable.

Not all KISS collectors collect KISS-related merchandise (i.e., records made by KISS members before they joined KISS or after they left KISS), but many do. Once collectors decide whether or not they want to have KISS-related merchandise, they may also decide which past or present members' related items they want to collect. Add $1–2 to any of the items if they are promotional.

RECORDS AND MERCHANDISE:
PAUL STANLEY, GENE SIMMONS,
BRUCE KULICK, ERIC SINGER (PRE-KISS)

PS/GS—*Wicked Lester* LP on bootleg audiotape. $7
PS/GS—*Wicked Lester* LP on bootleg LP (vinyl). $12–15
PS/GS—*Wicked Lester* LP on bootleg CD. $35–40
PS/GS—*Lyn Christopher* LP (Paul and Gene sing backup). $25
BK—*Great American Music* LP by Good Rats (one of Bruce's early bands). $6–8
BK—*Blackjack* LP by Blackjack (band that included Bruce Kulick and Michael Bolton, known then as Michael Bolotin). $8–10
BK—*Worlds Apart* LP by Blackjack. $8–10
BK—*Tale of the Tape* LP by Billy Squier (Bruce plays lead guitar). $5–6
ES—Badlands LPs that he performed on. $5–6

RECORDS AND MERCHANDISE:
ACE FREHLEY/FREHLEY'S COMET

Frehley's Comet (FC)—*Frehley's Comet* LP or cassette. $3–4
FC—*Second Sighting* LP or cassette. $2–3
FC—*Live + 1* LP or cassette. $2–3
AF—*Trouble Walkin'* LP or cassette. $3–4
45s or cassette singles from the above LPs. $4 each
12-inch Singles from the above LPs. $5 each
FC/AF—Album flats for any of the above LPs. $2 each

FC/AF—Promotional posters. $4–5
FC/AF—Any T-shirts from Ace's post-KISS career. $10–15 each
FC—Promotional deck of playing cards. $12

RECORDS AND MERCHANDISE: PETER CRISS, VINNIE VINCENT, MARK ST. JOHN

PC—*Chelsea* LP (pre-KISS). $25–30
PC—*Out of Control* LP or cassette (post-KISS). $10–12
PC—*Let Me Rock You* LP or cassette (post-KISS, only released in Europe). $12–15
VV—*Treasure* LP (pre-KISS). $20
VV—Any *Vinnie Vincent Invasion* LPs or cassettes. $2–3 each
VV—"Boys Wanna Rock" pink vinyl 45 (1st single by Vinnie Vincent Invasion). $8
MSJ—*White Tiger* LP or cassette. $2–3

INDEX

171